TRAINING RONIN STYLE

TRAINING RONIN STYLE
PRINCIPLES, TIPS, AND STRATEGIES FOR PRACTICAL MARTIAL ARTS SOLO PRACTICE

DAVID S. HOGSETTE

TRAINING RONIN STYLE
Principles, Tips, and Strategies for Practical Martial Arts Solo Practice

Copyright © 2020 David S. Hogsette

All rights reserved. Except for brief quotations in critical publications or reviews, no part of this book may be reproduced or utilized in any form or by any means, electronic or mechanical, including photocopying, recording, photographing, scanning, or by any storage or retrieval system, without prior written permission from the author.

ISBN-13: 979-8638379506

DISCLAIMER

The author and publisher of this material are NOT RESPONSIBLE in any manner whatsoever for any stress, duress, or injury which may occur through reading and practicing the techniques or following the instructions in this book. The activities, physical or otherwise, described in this book may be too strenuous or dangerous for some people, and the reader(s) should consult a physician before engaging in them.

DEDICATION

To Sensei Jerry Figgiani for his encouragement and support, commitment to the martial arts, and desire to share Okinawan karate with the world.

CONTENTS

	ACKNOWLEDGMENTS	ix
	INTRODUCTION	1
1	WHY SOLO TRAIN?	7
2	WARMING UP AND COOLING DOWN	17
3	KIHON AND PRACTICAL APPLICATION	25
4	KATA TRAINING AND BUNKAI	41
5	IMPACT TRAINING	59
6	COMBINING TRAINING METHODS	89
7	CARDIO AND STRENGTH TRAINING	99
	CONCLUSION	109
	BIBLIOGRAPHY	115
	ABOUT THE AUTHOR	117

ACKNOWLEDGMENTS

I would like to extend my deepest appreciation to the senseis and instructors with whom I have been training throughout these many years. Master Song Brown in Clarksville, TN, sparked my interest in Asian martial arts, teaching me Taekwondo while I was in high school. I am forever grateful to Senseis Richard and Jo McCulty of the Ohio State Karate Club who introduced me to Matsubayashi-ryu, training me to San Dan under the guidance and direction of Papas Paul Keller, Christopher Clarke, and Joe Hayes of the American Shorin-ryu Karate Association. I am grateful for the excellent instruction in Shotokan provided by Sensei Avi Azoulay, who trained me to Sho Dan. Thank you to Senseis Ryan and Chris McKenna of Shaolin Kempo Karate of Saint James for taking this ronin in and allowing me to train for several years, picking up some really cool combos, kempos, and forms. A special thank you to Iain Abernethy for introducing me to the growing, diverse, and enthusiastic world of practical karate. I first found his bunkai videos on YouTube and was immediately hooked. I have since participated in his seminars and continue to engage as much as possible through the Iain Abernethy online forum. I am thankful for his continued support and encouragement. I am especially thankful to Senseis Jerry Figgiani and Rick Kaufman of Shorin Ryu Karate Do International for bringing me back into the Matsubayashi-ryu fold, encouraging me in my exploration of practical bunkai, and hosting me in Okinawa to train in the honbu dojo with Senseis Tamaki and Tokashiki. A special shout out to Nate Herzog who served as uke for some of the bunkai application photos. Finally, I am so thankful for my beautiful and understanding wife, who tolerates my martial arts passion to such a degree that she agreed to be the photographer for this book. Xie xie!!

The Author with Sensei Tamaki in Okinawa, 2015

INTRODUCTION

Modern Day Ronin

Have you ever felt alone or adrift as a martial artist? Maybe you have moved to a new location and cannot find a dojo that matches the style or nature of the dojo you left. (No two dojos are ever alike, so if you try to find a dojo "just like" the one you left, you will be forever disappointed.) Maybe you are someone who drifts from dojo to dojo, taking a few classes from one instructor before moving on to the next. (I wouldn't advise such a strategy, as you will not learn very much about the different systems, you won't improve your skills markedly, and you will earn little respect from other martial artists.) Maybe you have a day job and don't own a dojo, but you are of advanced rank and you teach at your local YMCA or parks and recreation center two to three evenings during the week, but you do not have a more senior instructor in your area to be your sensei or instructor and to guide you further in your martial arts quest. (This is basically my own situation, and let me tell you, it's lonely and often discouraging.) Or, maybe there is a viral pandemic and your county or town is basically shut down, and you cannot go to your dojo and must train from home. (This apocalyptic scenario is not so farfetched, as this is exactly what happened with COVID-19 in the early part of 2020, as I finish writing this book.)

These are just a few examples of what I mean by modern day ronin. Literally, the term *ronin* in Japanese means wave man; that is, someone who is adrift without any stable mooring. Basically, a ronin is a vagrant or a wanderer. Historically, the term referred to feudal Japanese serfs who fled their master's lands and thus had no patron lord to whom he could give fealty in exchange for work, farmland, and protection. Such a status was, understandably, quite risky, lonely, and often life threatening.

Later, *ronin* referred to samurai who, for various reasons, no longer had a warlord master. A samurai would become ronin if his master were killed or if the master expelled the samurai from service, usually in disgrace. Samurai who lost their master were supposed to commit ceremonial suicide according to the samurai code of honor. Those who did not kill themselves became dishonored ronin, exiled in disgrace from the ranks of samurai. These ronin would wander in search of employment, some becoming hired swords, mercenaries, members of gangs, security for gambling establishments and brothels, or body guards for wealthy merchants. Others would become criminals, highway men robbing travelers, or pirates. There have been notable ronin in history, and some stories and films have even romanticized the ronin status. Generally speaking, however, ronin lived hard lives, mainly because they had no stable home and no secure master or lord to serve. Thus, they wandered in search of a new life to lead and new communities to join.

Hopefully, modern day ronin do not live such lives of desperation. If you find your life is similar to that of the ancient ronin, then seek help! All kidding aside, I refer to modern day ronin as karateka and other martial artists who, for whatever reason, find themselves without a sensei or instructor, or who have relocated far away from their sensei and cannot find a sensei and dojo in their new location, or who have decided to leave a particular dojo due to association politics or significant differences of opinion regarding training. Whatever the case may be, modern day ronin are karateka/martial artists who find themselves isolated and alone, but who still wish to train. I wrote this book for just such martial arts ronin.

Practical Karate or Applied Martial Arts

This book will be helpful to any karateka or martial artist, regardless of karate style or martial arts system. However, the training tips, strategies, and suggestions outlined in this book pertain mainly to practical karate or applied martial arts. If you are not a practical karateka or applied martial artists, have no fear! You need not stop reading at this point. These training tips pertain to you as well. Also, if you do not think of your martial arts training in the context of practical or applied martial arts, I hope this book will serve as a succinct primer or introduction to practical karate and applied martial arts.

So, what do I mean by practical karate and applied martial arts? Basically, it is karate and martial arts that can be applied in self-defense situations. Practical karate and applied martial arts explore tactics and techniques that are effective in actual confrontations "in the street." We should recognize that karateka and martial artists can train for a variety of contexts: martial arts (aesthetics of martial movements, power dynamics, history of combat, and culture), health and fitness (strengthening, weight loss, flexibility, coordination, improved balance, and enhanced concentration), self-improvement (concentration, confidence, self-esteem, health, general fitness, and personal accomplishment), sport and competition (kata performance, weapons demonstration, and point sparring), and self-defense (self-protection strategies and self-defense techniques). Practical karate and applied martial arts focus on the self-defense context.

Practical training for the self-defense context involves much more than learning and drilling combative techniques that will work in an actual self-defense confrontation. Such training should also focus on self-protection skills, including awareness, avoidance, de-escalation, ethical considerations (your combative abilities or skills versus your combative capabilities or what you are actually willing to do to another human being in the name of self-defense), legal issues (criminal and civil), body mechanics (effects of adrenaline on the body, generating power, human anatomy, vital targets, and joint manipulation), and articulation skills (how to explain your self-defense actions to lawyers, police investigators, and judges).

If you are unfamiliar with these self-protection principles, I highly recommend that you read such books as Peter Consterdine's *Streetwise: The Complete Manual of Personal Security and Self Defence*, Gavin De Becker's *The Gift of Fear: Survival Signals That Protect Us from Violence*, Lawrence Kane's and Kris Wilder's *The Little Black Book of Violence*, Rory Miller's *Facing Violence: Preparing for the Unexpected*, Rory Miller's *Meditations on Violence: A Comparison of Martial Arts Training and Real World Violence*, Rory Miller and Lawrence Kane's *Scaling Force: Dynamic Decision-Making Under Threat of Violence*, and Geoff Thompson's *Dead or Alive: The Choice is Yours*. There are many other books on the topic of self-protection, but these are excellent resources to begin your study.

In addition to self-protection skills, practical karate and applied martial arts training also includes learning and drilling self-defense tactics under the guidance of a qualified instructor involving plenty of partner training, impact training (striking pads and heavy bags), and live sparring (not point sparring or classical kumite but, rather, self-defense scenario sparring that simulates a self-defense situation). Practical karate and applied martial arts training must involve partner training.

However, solo training plays an important role, and this book explores solo training for modern ronin within the context of practical karate or applied martial arts. Again, if you do not usually train in practical karate or applied martial arts, don't worry! You will still find this book helpful to your particular solo training, and it may even peak your interest in practical martial arts. To learn more about practical karate and applied martial arts, browse the websites of these key figures: Iain Abernethy (iainabernethy.co.uk), Peter Consterdine (peterconsterdine.com), and Rory Miller (chirontraining.com).

My Own Martial Arts Journey

In the early 1980s I began martial arts training in Tae Kwon Do, and trained for three years. I began college in 1986, attending The Ohio State University. Desiring a more traditional martial art style, I started training in Matsubayashi Shorin-ryu with the Ohio State Karate Club. I joined the American Shorin-ryu Karate Association (ASKA), and I trained with Senseis Richard and Jo McCulty, under the guidance of Senseis Paul Keller, Chris Clarke, and Joe Hayes. In 1996 I graduated with a Ph.D. in English Language and Literature, and by that time I had achieved the rank of Ni Dan (2nd degree black belt) and was actively training for San Dan (3rd degree black belt). A few months later at an ASKA budo camp, I earned the rank of San Dan in Matsubayashi-ryu.

Through the ASKA, I established a strong Matsubayashi-ryu lineage. I was the student of Senseis Richard and Jo McCulty, who both trained directly under Sensei Paul Keller. Sensei Keller trained directly under Sensei Gary Tiktin, and he had the opportunity to train with Grandmaster Shoshin Nagamine and his son, Takayoshi Nagamine, along with such Shorin-ryu masters as Tadashi Yamashita and Chotoku Omine.

In 1996 I moved to Long Island, New York, to pursue a career as an English professor, and I trained for a year in Matsubayashi-ryu with Sensei Sal Franco. After moving around on Long Island, I began training in Shotokan, a Japanese martial arts with its roots in Okinawan Shorin-ryu. I trained with Sensei Avi Azoulay of the American Japanese Karate Association for about three years and earned a Sho Dan (1st degree black belt) in 2000.

As life would have it, I moved to another location on Long Island and could no longer train with Sensei Azoulay, and due to professional pressures, I had to stop training for several years. Then, in 2010, I began training with Senseis Ryan and Chris McKenna in Shaolin Kempo. In 2013, after finding Iain Abernethy's materials on YouTube, I became interested in practical self-defense applications of traditional karate, and in 2014, I subsequently returned to my Okinawan karate roots. I started training with Sensei Rick Kaufman and Sensei Jerry Figgiani, founder of Shorin Ryu Karate Do International (SRKDI). I joined SRKDI and have a lifetime dojo charter and am currently a member of the Board of Advisers.

In 2014, I moved to Grove City, PA, to be a professor of English and the Writing Program Director at Grove City College. I continue to train with Senseis Figgiani and Kaufman by attending SRKDI Doshi Kai training sessions and traveling with SRKDI yudansha (black belts) to Okinawa to train with Shorin-ryu masters. Through SRKDI, I have strengthened my Matsubayashi-ryu lineage. Sensei Figgiani has trained with some of the top instructors in Matsubayashi-ryu and Okinawan karate, including Takayoshi Nagamine, Kensei Taba, Joe Carbonara, Terry Maccarrone, Frank Grant, and Ernie Ferrara.

In 2017, I was promoted to Yon Dan (4th degree black belt) in Matsubayashi-ryu. My rank is officially recognized in Okinawa, through SRKDI and Shorin Ryu Karate Do International Okinawa, Naha-City, Okinawa, Japan. Through SRKDI's official relationship with Okinawa, I had the privilege of visiting and training in the Tokashiki Dojo, the SRKDI honbu or "home" dojo in Okinawa, where I was instructed by some of the highest ranking Okinawan masters who trained under Taba Sensei and Grandmaster Shoshin Nagamine, namely Sensei Takeshi Tamaki (Hanshi, 9th degree black belt) and Sensei Masahiko Tokashiki (Kyoshi, 8th degree black belt). I make every effort to return to Okinawa for continued training.

I have developed my practical karate experience by attending seminars with Iain Abernethy, one of the leading international figures in practical karate and bunkai training (kata analysis and application of techniques). I study his books and videos, and I am an active contributor to the forum on his website (iainabernethy.co.uk). Moreover, the videos and teachings of my sensei, Jerry Figgiani, further deepen my understanding of bunkai and practical application of karate. My study, practice, and training in Matsubayashi-ryu now focus on analyzing kata and kihon (basics) to develop effective self-defense tactics and techniques. While I do enjoy the martial arts context of karate training, my deep passion is for practical application. In that sense, I consider myself a true traditionalist in that I seek to explore the original heart and purpose of Okinawan karate—civilian combat and self-defense.

I started my own club at a local YMCA, the Shorin Ryu Karate Academy. I taught Matsubayashi-ryu from the practical karate perspective for a few years. I then offered a physical education karate class at Grove City College for two years. Unfortunately, due to budgetary constraints at the college, that course was cancelled. Now, I consider myself a practical karateka ronin, because I'm very far from my New York senseis and train primarily by myself. I try to reconnect with my senseis through training weekends and special doshi kai workshops, and I attend various training seminars as frequently as possible. But, for the moment, I'm mostly on my own. This book grows out of my training experiences as a practical karateka ronin. I hope you find this book helpful in your own ronin solo training.

The Author with Sensei Tokashiki in Okinawa, 2015

1 WHY SOLO TRAIN?

CIRCUMSTANCES NECESSITATING SOLO TRAINING

As already noted, optimal training for practical karate and applied martial arts involves partners. Ideally, we all should be training with an experienced sensei or instructor at a dojo or school that includes impact training, partner drills, live training, scenario training, and other related activities. Learning practical self-defense skills and training them adequately requires that we work with other practitioners in drills that involve varying degrees of compliance—high levels of compliance when we are first learning and practicing a technique through to low levels of compliance (even non-compliance) once we've gained proficiency in a technique and are trying to gain mastery so that we can apply the technique and its combative principles in a live self-defense situation. Partner training is indeed crucially necessary for effective practical karate and applied martial arts training.

However, there are circumstances in life that necessitate solo training. Most martial artists lead hectic lives, or travel for their work, or relocate for work or family related issues. Moreover, even if we find ourselves in a stable situation, training in a great dojo with an excellent sensei and other amazing karateka, solo training should still be a regular part of the applied martial artist's training regimen. The following is a brief list of circumstances that would necessitate solo training:

- Martial artists with a busy professional schedule that doesn't allow them to make it to the dojo regularly each week.

- Martial artists who travel extensively for their work and thus find themselves in various locations each week, making it impossible to attend regular training sessions in their home dojo.
- Students who have trained for many years in a great dojo environment but then move to a new location for whatever reason (family, career, education) and cannot find a suitable dojo nearby in which to continue training. Martial artists who started as children and achieved yudansha rank (black belt) and then go away to college, for example, often have a difficult time continuing their training. Solo practice can be an excellent way to supplement their training as they find a suitable dojo or martial arts club at the college or university.
- Instructors who are running a dojo but who do not have other senior students with whom to train advanced techniques, katas, and drills. Or, instructors who are continuing to develop their skills and knowledge, which every instructor on principle should do anyway. As Sensei Jerry Figgiani, founder and president of Shorin Ryu Karate Do International, explains, "The great thing about the study of the martial arts is that it always gives us a new opportunity to take ourselves to another level."[1] Solo training enhances the instructor's ability to set personal training goals and to explore specific aspects of the martial arts.
- Students who are happy with their dojo environment, but who want to expand or supplement their training, particularly in the area of applied karate. (Note, solo training can only take you so far in the area of practical martial arts, as partner training is essential to develop skills in self-defense and civil combat.)
- Karateka and martial artists who have trained in a dojo specializing in competition and martial arts contexts and who wish to delve more into applied martial arts. Such martial artists can supplement their dojo training with practical solo training as they look for a suitable dojo to develop their new interest in applied martial arts.
- Students eager to enhance their dojo training with personalized individual training so as to practice their techniques outside of class.
- Advanced karateka and martial artists who are interested in exploring their martial art in greater depth and to make the elements of their system their own.

---

[1] Fraguas, *Karate Masters*, p. 22.

Solo training will help martial artists in any of these situations. Moreover, even if you train in a great dojo with an excellent sensei, you can still benefit from solo training. Your sensei or instructor develops a training curriculum with all his/her students in mind, and the instructor determines the given focus of any class. Sometimes, that focus may not totally relate to you as an individual practitioner (though, you will still benefit from that class session). Working solo allows you to take responsibility for your own training. The strategies outlined in this book will help all martial artists supplement their training, particularly in the areas of applied martial arts.

Solo Training is Purely Supplemental

As outlined above, there are many reasons for solo training. However, let me emphasize that in no way am I suggesting that solo practice can substitute for training in a dojo, under the supervision of a sensei. Moreover, I am not suggesting that solo training can replace partner training. For any martial arts, but especially for practical karate and applied martial arts, partner training is essential. You have to practice the self-defense techniques and kata bunkai first with compliant partners and then, as your skill increases, against less-compliant partners. Eventually, you need to train your skills live, engaging "all in" sparring (observing reasonable safety protocols, of course). I am not suggesting that solo training, by itself, is a complete and sufficient form of training. No way.

The Bubishi, an ancient Chinese text that informed the creation of Okinawan karate, illustrates the ways in which martial arts training requires working with a partner. Indeed, kata or forms were created as a method of solo training to practice the various self-defense techniques when one could not engage partner training, and the various forms and kata served as a physical training tool that encapsulated the combative principles and self-defense techniques of a given martial arts system or of the person who created the kata. These kata were intended as a supplement, not a replacement, for partner training.

The tips, strategies, and recommendations in this book outline a variety of solo training practices. I am not suggesting that one can be a successful martial artist by engaging in solo training only. That is impossible. Practical karate or applied martial arts is truly traditional in the sense that it views karate as it was originally intended: a system of civilian combat that is effective against ruffians and criminals. In order for training in practical karate to be effective in meeting its original purposes—training the individual for self-defense and civilian combat—the practitioner must work with other karateka, engaging in partner training, live sparring drills, and pressure testing his/her techniques against non-compliant partners. Solo practice alone cannot provide this essential training element.

The point of this book is to aid practical karateka and applied martial artists in developing and enhancing their solo training as a *supplement* to partner training. Solo training should never replace training with other practitioners in a dojo, under the direction of a skilled and knowledgeable sensei. Rather, solo training is a supplement, allowing the karateka or martial artist to focus on exploring, developing, and refining practical martial arts skills learned in the dojo. Solo training should never replace partner training; rather, it is a supplement that strengthens and supports working with partners.

LIMITATIONS AND BENEFITS OF SOLO TRAINING

Solo training should never replace partner training because of its significant limitations:

- **No feedback from a partner.** Working with another person offers the opportunity to receive immediate feedback on your techniques. When working with partners, you can develop timing, speed, focus, and, to some extent, power. You can determine the effectiveness of your techniques, and you can test the efficacy of your bunkai applications (interpretations of movements in kata as self-defense tactics).
- **Working with a partner sharpens your BS filters.** You can develop interesting interpretations of kata movements, but you cannot know if they really work or not unless you "field test" your techniques. Solo training does not offer this kind of feedback that is essential for practical karate or applied martial arts training.
- **Developing an isolated training bubble.** If you only train by yourself, you can develop a self-limiting training bubble in which you receive no feedback or instruction. You can easily develop counterproductive bad habits without realizing it, and then you reinforce them through uncorrected repetition. You can also develop a false sense of assurance in your skills. Your techniques may *feel* impressive, they may *feel* like they are effective, and they me *seem* reasonable to you, but unless you train them with a non-compliant

partner, you will never really know if your techniques are effective (unless you end up having to use them in a real confrontation, and by that time, you had better hope your techniques are effective, because your life may depend upon it). Solo training exclusively can potentially lead you down a path of destruction, because it is likely you will develop a confidence in techniques that may actually get you hurt or even killed in a real confrontation.

Although solo training by itself in the absence of a sensei's instruction and partner training can ultimately be counterproductive, that does not mean it is totally worthless. Indeed, there are several benefits to solo training, as long as it is a supplement to and not a replacement for your dojo and partner training:

- **Flexibility.** Solo training is totally flexible, and can be adjusted to your own schedule. Dojo training is set by the sensei, and you have to alter your own schedule in order to make the classes. Solo training is completely flexible, dependent only upon your own work schedule, family obligations, and lifestyle choices. You can solo train whenever you have a few minutes to spare or an hour or more.
- **Self-determined pace.** When training in the dojo, the sensei sets the pace, determining how long the class spends on specific activities. When you train by yourself, you are the sensei, and you can decide how long you spend working certain techniques. The sensei has a whole class to consider, and he/she is moving the students through a set curriculum. The sensei has a responsibility to each of the students to make sure progress is made. However, when you train solo, you can determine how long you spend on certain techniques and combative principles.
- **Focus on your own training goals.** In a dojo training context, the sensei determines the curriculum, organizes the training sessions, and establishes goals for the students. When you train on your own, you can determine your specific training goals. Ideally, you should use the solo training to supplement, reinforce, and deepen your dojo and partner training. However, solo training can also be an opportunity for you to focus on techniques and concepts not fully explored in your dojo experience. For example, if your dojo doesn't analyze kata or forms or practice practical bunkai drills, you can do so on your own in your solo training. Of course, such solo practice will be limited, because you still need to drill your practical

techniques with compliant partners and test the techniques with live, non-compliant partners. Nevertheless, solo training allows you to train beyond what is covered in the dojo and to pursue your own training goals.

- **Engage full power training.** When you train in a dojo, you must consider the safety and health of your training partners. Generally speaking, everyone in the dojo has a day job, a family, and societal obligations. You cannot hurt each other each night in the dojo. Therefore, you must use proper control when training with partners. Even if you are using safety equipment, you still cannot go "all out" against your partner. However, when solo training and using impact equipment, you can punch, kick, and strike as hard as you possibly can. You can work on power and develop really devastating techniques by practicing against a heavy bag, a target dummy, and other such impact training equipment.

Adjusting Training to Space Limits and Time Constraints

Because solo training is so flexible, you literally can adapt it to any schedule or lifestyle, be it hectic, slow paced, or fluctuating between these two extremes. When developing your own solo training regimens, be sure to recognize training opportunities in what may seem like limitations. If you've trained extensively in a dojo, you may think that you need a large space in which to train. Not so! You can shadow box, practice kicks, and execute countless punches and blocks and strikes from a side stance in a very small space. You don't need to march up and down a large room practicing techniques.

If you are on a business trip, you can watch the news or your favorite TV show in your hotel room while practicing strikes in whatever stance you choose. If you have a garage, a basement, or a guest room in your house, you can convert some of that space into a small training area. Live in a cramped apartment? No worries. Your living room space, or a second bedroom/office, or the eat-in kitchen area can serve as a temporary training space. In nice weather, you can train outside in your yard, a public park, a grassy area or recreation space in your apartment complex, or your deck or patio. If you live in an apartment complex that provides a gym or workout room, see if you can use that space for your solo training. If your place of employment has a gym or conference rooms that are unused for specific blocks of time (particularly during lunch hour), see if you can use those areas for solo training. If you are a college student, professor, or staff member, seek out gym space, empty rooms, racket ball courts, or basketball court space in the campus gym or recreation center during off times (lunch time, late afternoon, and evening) where you can solo train.

The objective is to find any workable space wherever you happen to be so that you can solo train. For example, when my wife and I visit family in China, we usually stay with her parents. They live in a housing and apartment development with outdoor public exercise spaces. I use these public areas to get in some solo training whenever possible (sometimes to the delight and curiosity of neighbors and passersby who gather to watch the Westerner practice Eastern martial arts).

Figure 1: Outdoor Training Area in China   *Figure 2: Outdoor Training Area in China*

Finding time to solo train is a whole other challenge. We all lead very busy lives, and we convince ourselves that we don't have time for solo training. But is that necessarily true? Many of us are used to thinking that we need long blocks of time to train; however, you can get a great workout in 20-30 minutes. Or, you can do a 10-15 minute workout in the morning and one in the evening. If you are traveling on a business trip, you can get a quick workout in at the hotel gym, or in your hotel room. Again, limited space doesn't necessarily matter.

You can complete an excellent karate or martial arts workout in a limited space, just by executing strikes and kicks from a stationary stance, like a fighting stance or a side stance. You can also perform kata in a small area by readjusting your position after two or three moves. The point is to practice the movements, think about their application, and work up a sweat. You don't need a whole bunch of space or time to do that. If you commit yourself to finding space and time to train, and if you have a bit of imagination, you can make time and find adequate space for productive solo training.

You can also take advantage of some unconventional training opportunities. Do you have a dog that needs to be walked two or three times per day? Why not run with the dog instead of just walking? Do you work on the fifth floor of an office building? Take the stairs instead of the elevator. Live in an apartment building on the third floor? Why not jog up every time you return home? Do you have stairs in your home? If you cannot train or get to the gym or dojo, consider running up and down the stairs for 15-20 minutes, or do lunges on the first few steps for 20 minutes, or doing pushups and planks with your feet on the fourth or fifth step and your hands on the floor level.

Sure, these exercises mainly focus on cardio and strength without performing or practicing your karate or martial arts techniques, but they can still supplement your dojo training and other solo martial arts training. Some kind of training is better than no training at all, even if it isn't specifically a karate or martial arts workout. Being a modern ronin requires some imagination, creativity, and flexibility. Contemplate your situation, your lifestyle, where you live, and where you work, and develop specific training routines that will help you pursue your training goals and supplement your dojo training.

What Past Traditions and Masters Have Said

Solo practice has always been an important element of martial arts training. Indeed, it has been universally known that in order to develop practical fighting skills, one must train with partners who exhibit varying degrees of compliance. Despite the centrality of partner training to the martial arts, solo practice has always been considered a significant, even necessary, component of martial training.

Evidence of solo practice can be seen in ancient Chinese martial arts training manuals, dating back to the Chinese Ming Dynasty (the sixteenth century AD). Paintings and references to solo martial training in China date back to as early as the second century BC. Such training manuals and paintings of martial activities depict both partner drills and solo practice; moreover, the Chinese considered martial training to be highly individualistic, believing people should practice at their own pace, according to the dictates of their body types and qi (life force). Thus, training often took place in small groups, usually one-on-one with teacher and student, and included significant amounts of solo practice.[2]

Martial arts training in Okinawa, which was heavily influenced by Chinese martial practices, also involved small groups, usually a sensei or karate master teaching a few students in his home. Partner drills, individual kata training, and solo conditioning were the main elements of Okinawan martial practice. We do not have many historical documents from ancient Okinawan culture, and many of the few historical documents that did exist were destroyed during the bombings of Okinawa in World War II. However, the writings of some modern masters reveal the importance of solo training to traditional karate.

For example, Anko Itosu (1831-1915), commonly referred to as the grandfather of modern karate (Gichin Funakoshi being the father of modern karate), briefly explains the necessity of individual makiwara training in the fourth of his ten precepts of karate: "In karate, training of the hands and feet are important, so you should train thoroughly with a sheaf of straw [makiwara]. In order to do this, drop your shoulders, open your lungs, muster your strength, grip the floor with your feet, and concentrate your energy into your lower abdomen. Practice using each arm one to two hundred times each day."[3]

Choki Motobu (1870-1944), a student of Itosu, explains in his book *Okinwan Kempo* how to make a traditional makiwara training device and illustrates various solo makiwara drills.[4] Gichin Funakoshi (1868-1957), another prominent student of Itosu who took Shorin-ryu to mainland Japan and renamed it Shotokan, illustrates solo kihon and kata training in his foundational books *Karate-Do Nyumon* and *Karate-Do Kyohan*.

Finally, Shoshin Nagamine (1907-1997), founder of Matsubayashi Shorin-ryu, provides pictorial outlines in his book *The Essence of Okinawan Karate-Do* of all eighteen kata of his system, the main content of solo practice at the heart of Matsubayashi Shorin-ryu. And, in his chapter on kumite (sparring with a partner), he explains some key individual conditioning training exercises and drills intended to strengthen and prepare the individual for partner training.[5]

---

[2] For further analysis of the history of martial training as depicted in Chinese training manuals from antiquity to the modern era, see Kennedy and Guo, *Chinese Martial Arts Training Manuals*.
[3] Itosu, "The 10 Precepts of Anko Itosu."
[4] Motobu, *Okinawan Kempo*, 41-51.
[5] Nagamine, *The Essence of Okinawan Karate-Do*, 103-265.

Conclusion

These are just a few examples from Chinese and Okinawan martial arts history illustrating the central importance of solo training. Karate masters of old recognized that partner drills are essential to developing proficiency in combative skills. However, they also recognized that this partner training should be supplemented with dynamic, engaging, and practical solo practice that augments and enhances the purposes and goals of partner training.

Building upon the spirit of the ancient Chinese training manuals and the books and precepts from modern Okinawan karate masters, this book provides specific examples, strategies, and tips for contemporary martial artists who are interested in enhancing their martial arts practice with effective, practical, and fun solo training drills.

Figure 3: Outdoor Training Area in China. When my wife and I visit China, we usually stay with her parents, who live in a large housing complex with a variety of open spaces that I use for solo training. Most Chinese families enjoy outdoor activities, and some stop to watch the curious sight of a Western foreigner practicing Eastern martial arts.

2 WARMING UP AND COOLING DOWN

Principles of Warming Up

All athletes, be they professional or amateur, recognize the value and necessity of warming up before engaging in serious training. Yet, a variety of theories raise important questions about warming up: What constitutes an effective warmup session? How long should athletes warm up? What is the relationship between warming up and cooling down? What role does stretching play in the warmup? What are the differences between dynamic stretching and static stretching, and when should athletes engage these types of stretching activities? Exercise fads come and go, and it can be difficult to know which theories are the most beneficial. Ultimately, we have to try different exercises and decide what works best for ourselves, given our unique bodies, activities, strengths, weaknesses, and training goals.

Concerning warmup exercises for karate training, Shoshin Nagamine, founder of Matsubayashi Shorin-ryu, explains in his book *The Essence of Okinawan Karate-Do* that the central importance of warming up is to "loosen muscles, joints, and all parts of the body. The warmup exercises also increase blood circulation and help to prevent the student from being injured because of strained muscles, or unreadiness for speedy movements. Any physical exercises from sports or other martial arts may be added to the warmup when necessary."[1] I follow these basic principles when developing my own training warmup exercises, and I appreciate Master Nagamine's openness to integrating a variety of exercises from other sports or martial arts. Basically, experiment with different warmup principles and examples, and develop what works best for you.

---

[1] Nagamine, *Essence of Okinawan Karate-Do*, 51.

A good warmup routine should be structured with the following physiological principles in mind:

- **Activity to increase the heart rate and raise the body temperature.** Get your heart pumping and break a little sweat. You can also use this warm-up time to get in a little cardio workout. Of course, you'll want more cardio than just a few minutes during warmup, but why not include cardio exercise as part of your warmup routine?
- **Activity to loosen and warm up the joints.** Martial arts training can be stressful on the joints, so make sure your warmup routine sufficiently engages, loosens, and warms your joints. Loosening and warming the joints are particularly important for older martial artists, but younger practitioners should also get into the habit of warming up the joints to avoid injury and to maintain joint health as they age.
- **Dynamic stretching.** Recent exercise science studies indicate that dynamic stretching before sport activity is more beneficial than static stretching, and that static stretching is best engaged after activity.[2] Be sure to incorporate effective dynamic stretching in your warm-up routine.
- **Further activity to increase heart rate and body temperature.** End your warm-up with activity relevant to your training goals that will further increase heart rate and body temperature such that all the major muscle groups and joints are sufficiently warmed up and ready to engage your training regimen.

TRADITIONAL WARMUP

All traditional martial arts systems have a set of warmup activities commonly used to prepare practitioners for training. If you are part of a martial arts school or have been training in a traditional style for many years, review the regular warmup activities and design your own warmup that meets the physiological principles listed and discussed above. Here is an example of a traditional warmup routine for Matsubayashi-ryu:

---

[2] For example, see Danny McMillan, et. al., "Dynamic vs. Static-Stretching Warm Up."

1. A minute or so of jumping jacks (increases heart rate and body temperature).
2. Several repetitions of head rotations, such as looking left and right, looking up and down, tilting the head left and right, and rotating the head to the left and then to the right (warms the neck joints).
3. Rolling the shoulders forward and then backward (warms the shoulder joints).
4. Arm rotations forward and to the rear (warms the shoulder joints) (**Figure 1**).
5. Crossing your arms in front and reaching to the rear (ballistic stretching and warming of the shoulders, chest, and upper back).
6. Rotating from the waist, twisting to the left and to the right, usually in a side stance (warms the lower back, hips, and waist area).
7. Leaning to the left and to the right while punching over the head to each side, usually in a side stance (ballistic stretching of the waist, sides, shoulders, and arms) (**Figure 2**).
8. Leaning forward to touch the floor and leaning backward, looking up at the ceiling (ballistic stretching of the lower back, hamstrings, abdomen, and front of hips).
9. Straight leg lifts to the front (ballistic stretching of the hamstrings).
10. Straight leg lifts to the rear (ballistic stretching of the front of the hips and the quadriceps).
11. Straight leg lifts to the side (ballistic stretching of the hips and inner thigh).
12. Several sets of punching in side stance (further activity to increase heart rate and body temperature).

Figure 1

Figure 2

Practical, Combative, and Context-Specific Warmup

In addition to using traditional warmup routines, you can also consider developing your own warmup based upon practical self-defense techniques, combative principles, or context-specific training activities. Reflect upon the techniques you plan to practice in a given training session and devise a warmup that engages the body movements, combative principles, and self-defense techniques you plan to train during that session. For example, if you are warming up for some impact training that involves hand, elbow, knee, and kicking techniques, you might devise a warm-up routine like the following:

1. A minute round jumping rope or jumping jacks (increases heart rate and body temperature).
2. A minute round jumping back forth (left and right) over the straightened rope or an imaginary line (increases heart rate and body temperature) (**Figure 3**).
3. A minute round of light shadow boxing using hand and elbow techniques only, making sure you use practical techniques that pertain to the context for which you are training, like point sparring or street self-defense (warms the shoulder, elbow, and wrist joints).
4. A minute round leaning to the left and to the right while punching over the head to each side (ballistic stretching of the waist, sides, shoulders, and arms).
5. A minute round of light shadow boxing using knee and kicking techniques only (warms the hips, knees, and ankle joints) (**Figure 4**).
6. A minute round of knee raises to the front and to the side (ballistic stretching of the hips and warming of the hip joints).
7. A minute round of leg raises to the front, rear, and side (ballistic stretching of the hamstrings, front of the hips, and inner thighs).
8. A minute round of light and/or moderate shadow boxing, involving hand, elbow, knee, and kicking techniques (further relevant activity to increase heart rate and body temperature).

Figure 3    *Figure 4*

If you are planning to practice kihon techniques (basics of blocking, stricking, and kicking) and kata (pre-arranged forms), you might devise a warmup routine like the following:

1. A minute round of running in place or jogging on a treadmill (increases heart rate and body temperature).
2. A minute round of lunges (increases heart rate and body temperature while ballistically stretching the hips and hamstrings used in the front stance).
3. A minute round of squat jacks, moving the arms downward as you squat down into the side stance and moving the arms upward as you straighten the legs (increases heart rate and body temperature as you warm the shoulders, hips, and knee joints) (**Figure 5**).
4. Several reps of light high blocks as you squat down into side stance (warms the shoulders, hips, and knee joints).
5. Several reps of light chest blocks as you squat down into side stance (warms the shoulders, elbows, hips, and knee joints).
6. Several reps of light low blocks as you step forward, lunging into front stance (warms the shoulders, elbows, hips, and knee joints and ballistically stretches the hamstrings).
7. Several reps of light low blocks sliding left and right in side stance (warms shoulders, elbows, hips, knee joints, and inner thighs (**Figure 6**).

8. Several sets of punching in side stance (further activity to increase heart rate and body temperature).

Figure 5

Figure 6

Another option for a kihon and kata workout warmup, particularly if you are short on time, would be to intersperse one-minute rounds of jogging in place (or light jogging on a treadmill) and/or jumping rope with one or two kata, performed at a moderate speed. Again, the idea is to warm up the relevant joints and muscles, elevate the body temperature, and prepare your body and mind for your specific workout session.

COOLING DOWN

After each training session, you should plan a brief cooldown period lasting at least five to ten minutes. Your cooldown can be as diverse and relevant as your warmup, and it should accomplish at least two key goals:
1. lowering heart rate and body temperature gradually and
2. increasing flexibility through static stretching.

Yoga stretching has become increasingly more popular in the West, and you may consider incorporating some basic yoga stretches into your cooldown routine.

If you were impact training, you might consider cooling down with a few rounds of light punching and kicking on the heavy bag, followed by a few rounds of light shadow boxing, and finishing with several minutes of static stretching of large muscle groups.

If you were training kata and kihon, you might consider cooling down by performing a few basic kata (or the latest kata you are working on) in slow motion, focusing on form and technique, followed by a few repetitions of basic kihon techniques in appropriate stances for your style (like walking stance and/or front stance, moving up and down the floor), followed by a few sets of light punches in side stance, and ending with several minutes of static stretching of large muscle groups.

Conclusion

Whatever your specific training session happens to be, make sure you begin with a carefully considered warmup routine that prepares you for the training to come, and end with a purposeful cooldown session that gradually lowers your heart rate and body temperature, using techniques and body movements consistent with the training session. Also, don't forget to end all training sessions with relevant static stretching exercises that condition the joints, muscles, and connective tissues associated with the techniques and body movements you practiced during that session.

The Author with Sensei Jerry Figgiani in Okinawa, 2015

3 KIHON TRAINING AND PRACTICAL APPLICATION

Repetitive practice of basic techniques known as kihon is a fundamental part of traditional martial arts training. Contemporary students who are new to traditional martial arts often find kihon training dull, boring, and uninspiring—they want to get straight to the sparring! However, you cannot learn to fight, spar, or defend yourself unless you can perform the basic techniques of fighting. Kihon training teaches you the necessary skill sets to become successful in kata (forms) training, sparring (sport karate), and self-defense (fighting to escape).

Shoshin Nagamine, the founder of Matsybayashi Shorin-ryu, explains, "The basic movements are the fundamental defensive and offensive movements of karate. The karate student must practice these fundamentals thoroughly until they become an instinctive part of his own character. To train the body properly, constant repetition of each movement is required."[1] Similarly, Gichin Funakoshi, the man who introduced Shorin-ryu to mainland Japan and called it Shotokan, notes, "Before practicing the kata, learn well how to stand and how to kick. In order to move freely within the kata, one should practice, as part of the regular basic training (*kihon*), those techniques and stances that occur most frequently in the kata."[2]

Repetition of the basics is essential for progressing in the martial arts, and since kihon practice is by nature individual and does not require a partner, you can easily incorporate it into your personal training regimen. Consider the following when developing your own kihon training sessions:

1. Review your strengths and weaknesses and develop kihon training routines that quickly review your strong techniques while leaving

---

[1] Nagamine, *The Essence of Okinawan Karate-Do*, p. 56.
[2] Funakoshi, *Karate-Do Kyohan: The Master Text*, p. 29.

more time to focus on your weaker kihon or the techniques you have recently learned.
2. If possible, practice in front of a mirror or a reflective window (dark outside and light inside) so that you can evaluate and correct your techniques. Many gyms have multipurpose rooms outfitted with mirrors—try to schedule your kihon training sessions when those rooms are available for general membership use. I try to use the multipurpose room or the dance studio at the college where I teach.
3. Find large spaces in which to train so that you can incorporate movement into your kihon practice. Try to use your gym's multipurpose room, arena, or intramural space during open training times. Use your garage or basement space. Train in your backyard or driveway when weather permits. Practice your kihon in a public park or your apartment complex's courtyard. When my wife and I visit family in China, I use different courtyard spaces throughout the housing complex where we usually stay. You'd be surprised just how many open spaces there are to utilize for your kihon training.
4. If you have limited space (small apartment, hotel room, your bedroom, or a corner in your office), practice your kihon in stationary stances. You can get a great kihon workout by performing all your basic blocks, punches, and other strikes from the side stance or horse-riding stance. You can practice kicks and knee strikes from walking stance, fighting stance, forward stance, cat stance, and back stance. If you have a bit more space to work with, you can incorporate minimal movement in these stances, using slide up stepping, lunging movements, lead-leg shifts, and drop stepping. This strategy works really well when on business trips—you can watch TV in your hotel room as you bust out some kihon in side stance.
5. If you have sufficient room to train, then you can always engage in traditional kihon sets, moving up and down the floor as in the dojo. Simply copy how your sensei or martial arts instructor structures kihon or basics training in your dojo or training space. As you practice, be sure to check your stances and form periodically, serving as your own personal sensei or trainer.
6. In addition to mimicking traditional kihon practice, you can also liven up your basic training a bit with one-minute rounds. Download a basic interval timer onto your smartphone and program it for a specific number of one-minute rounds with ten seconds of rest between each round. Depending upon your current physical

condition, get in as many repetitions of a particular technique during each round. Consider a medium pace for the first half of the round and then full speed and power for the second half of the round, thus working form and technique in addition to good cardio training and pushing yourself to fight through exhaustion. Ten to fifteen minutes of such circuit training will certainly get your heart pumping and the sweat dripping.

KIHON AND PRACTICAL KARATE

In modern martial arts, traditional kihon or basic training has received a poor reputation, largely due to some misconceptions. Practitioners of combat-oriented martial arts have told me that kihon is impractical, because no one fights that way in real life. They ask, "Who fights with one hand on the hip, and who marches around blocking over his/her head with the other hand doing nothing back in the chamber?"

These are fair questions, but unfortunately, most modern martial artists treat these questions as rhetorical, rarely waiting for the answer. By asking the question, they are actually making a dismissive claim about the ineffectiveness and impracticality of such kihon. Sadly, many such martial artists have come to believe there are no reasonable answers to these questions, because they have not encountered many traditional martial artists who can provide the answers.

Kihon training in its traditional form actually is quite practical, and the techniques as typically performed have effective self-defense applications—if you know how to interpret and apply the techniques. Let's not forget that karate and other traditional martial arts were created and evolved in response to real violence within specific historical and cultural contexts. Practitioners of these traditional martial arts have been practicing these techniques for hundreds of years and more, and traditional practitioners continue training this way today not simply because of tradition but because it is practical and effective.

For example, anyone who has trained in a fighting art knows that power in techniques largely depends upon a person's strength. This is undeniable. A big, strong person, all other things being equal, will punch harder than a smaller, weaker person. However, experienced martial artists also understand that size and strength are not the *sole* determiners of power. Speed, proper form, body dynamics, relaxation, tension, hip movement, joint and limb alignment, striking surface area, timing, dynamics of breathing, and other such elements all factor into the power of a technique. All things not being equal, a smaller, weaker person with amazing speed and well-developed form can strike much harder than a larger, stronger person with poor form. Repetitive kihon training develops proper form, body dynamics, speed, hip movement, and all the other intricacies that go into hard, fast, powerful techniques. In other words, traditional kihon training is practical in that it helps you develop strong and effective fighting techniques through repetition and refining body mechanics (**Figure 1**).

In addition to developing good form, speed, and power, kihon training, when engaged correctly, also develops practical self-defense techniques that are effective in real-life contexts. That hand pulled back to the side or on the hip ("back in the pocket") is NOT a dead hand doing nothing. Rather, that position represents hikite or grabbing and pulling a limb or other body part of the opponent. The hand is closed to represent grabbing with that hand. And, the palm is facing upward to indicate that you have not only pulled but also twisted the limb, as your hand moves from palm down when extending and grabbing to palm up when pulling and twisting (**Figure 2**).

Figure 1: Low Block Kihon

Figure 2: Low Block Kihon Application

Practicing kihon with this understanding of extended and retracted limbs helps us realize that the traditional kihon techniques are actually effective in-close fighting strategies. Those punches with the one hand extended and the other hand in the chamber is actually punching in a clinch scenario in which you are pulling the opponent into your punches or clearing limbs out of the way to create a path to your target. Those high blocks with one hand over your head and the other back in the chamber position may actually not be a block at all; rather, you have cleared a guard and pulled it down and away from the enemy's head as you thrust your forearm into the throat, side of the neck, or jawline. When we approach training from this self-defense application perspective, we see that kihon practice can actually be very practical indeed!

When you practice your traditional kihon, be sure to visualize the various practical applications associated with each basic technique. Review what your sensei or martial arts instructor has taught you about applying the kihon technique in practical ways. If your martial arts school does not discuss or teach practical application, then do your own research. Many excellent instructors are writing books, producing DVDs, posting YouTube videos, and conducting training seminars demonstrating practical application of kihon and kata (forms). Take the time to study these materials and incorporate them into your kihon training.[3]

When I train my kihon techniques, I usually pair traditional practice with practical application training. First, I will execute ten repetitions (or a minute round, depending upon that day's routine) of a technique in the traditional kihon method typically used in my style of Matsubayashi Shorin-ryu, visualizing various practical applications. Then, I will execute ten repetitions (or a minute round) of shadow boxing in which I visualize using that particular technique in a clinch scenario or some other self-defense context. I then move to the next kihon technique, practicing it in the traditional style visualizing an application, followed by practical application shadow boxing. During the shadow boxing, I may also include a variety of follow-up techniques as I fight to escape the imagined attacker.

The following list is a simple example of a basic kihon training session in which you work the traditional technique paired with practical application shadow boxing. There are many possible applications for each of these kihon techniques. This list serves as merely one example of how you might apply these traditional techniques in a self-defense scenario. You can do multiple sets each or work them in minute rounds, depending upon your training goals and allocated time for training.

1. Lunge Punches

Traditional Kihon: Lunge punch in walking stance (**Figure 3**) or front stance (**Figure 4**), stepping up and down the floor.

---

[3] I highly recommend the work of Jerry Figgiani, founder and president of Shorin Ryu Karatedo International (www.srkdi.com) and Iain Abernethy, the chief international coach for the World Combat Association (www.iainabernethy.com). Also check out the work of Vince Morris, founder of Kissaki-Kai Karate (www.kissakikarate.com), and Don Came, senior instructor for Kissaki-Kai Karate (www.doncame.com). I also have dozens of training videos on my website (www.shorinryukarate.club)—click the videos tab and browse away!

Figure 3

Figure 4

Practical Application Shadow Boxing: From a simulated clinch position in a basic fighting stance, check and grab a hook punch (**Figure 5**), pull down and back in hikite as you punch with the other hand (**Figure 6**). Strike repeatedly or throw in some knees and elbows and back away with your hands up in a defensive position.[4] Switch your feet and repeat on the other side.

Figure 5

Figure 6

---

[4] When working self-defense drills of any kind, you should practice backing away in a defensive manner, looking around for other potential enemy attacks. Evading and escaping is a skill that needs to be practiced. Also, such practice reduces the risk of developing poor drilling habits of stepping back in to work the other side. In the street, you want to escape, not step back in for another go at the technique.

2. High Blocks

Traditional Kihon: High block in walking stance (**Figure 7**) or front stance (**Figure 8**), stepping up and down the floor.

Figure 7

Figure 8

Practical Application Shadow Boxing: From a simulated clinch position in a basic fighting stance, imagine the attacker has grabbed your lapel and attempts to punch you with his other hand. Reach up and seize his hand that has grabbed your lapel (this is the hikite hand) and stuff his attempted punch with your other hand, pushing his arm down and against his body. Quickly jam your forearm into the crook of his arm that is holding your lapel (**Figure 9**: windup for the high block) and immediately thrust your forearm into his throat (**Figure 10**: high block motion) as you pull down and back on the hand you have grabbed (hikite). Strike his throat multiple times, follow up with some elbows and knee strikes, and back away with your hands up in a defensive position. Switch your feet and repeat on the other side.

Figure 9

Figure 10

3. Outside Chest Blocks

Traditional Kihon: Outside chest block (moving the arm from the inside to the outside) in walking stance (**Figure 11**) or front stance (**Figure 12**), stepping up and down the floor.

Figure 11

Figure 12

Practical Application Shadow Boxing: From a simulated clinching position, use the hand that is around the back of the enemy's neck to strike the back of the attacker's neck with the inside of the wrist or forearm. Reach around and grab his chin (**Figure 13**: windup for the chest block) and use the chest-block motion to pull his head around and twist his body (**Figure 14**: chest-block position). Follow up with various strikes to his head and/or neck and back away with your hands up in a defensive position. Switch your feet and repeat on the other side.

Figure 13

Figure 14

4. Inside Chest Blocks

Traditional Kihon: Inside chest block (arm moves from outside to inside) in walking stance, stepping up and down the floor (**Figures 15-16**).

Figure 15

Figure 16

Practical Application Shadow Boxing: The attacker is reaching in to choke you, gouge your eyes, or grab you. Parry his reach and grab his wrist with your other hand, ending in a cross grab (**Figure 17**). Use the hikite to pull his arm, stretching out his arm and pulling him forward off balance. Immediately thrust your other forearm into the outside of the elbow joint of his straightened arm, attacking the joint or applying an arm bar (**Figure 18**). Follow up with some strikes and back away with your hands up in a defensive position. Switch your feet and repeat on the other side.

Figure 17

Figure 18

5. Low Blocks

Traditional Kihon: Low block in front stance, moving up and down the floor (**Figures 19-20**).

Practical Application Shadow Boxing: From a simulated clinch position, throw a few elbow strikes to enemy's head (**Figure 21**) and imagine he has pulled both arms up to cover his head. With the elbowing arm, reach around and hit the back of his head with your forearm. Reach further around and grab the enemy's face or chin (windup for the "block") and pull it down, disrupting his posture and creating an opening to his head (**Figure 22**). Strike several time to the head and back away with your hands up in a defensive position. Switch your feet and repeat on the other side.

Figure 19

Figure 20

Figure 21

Figure 22

6. Shuto (Knife-Hand) Blocks

Traditional Kihon: Shuto (knife-hand) blocks in cat stance (or back stance), moving up and down the floor (**Figures 23-24**).

Figure 23

Figure 24

Practical Application Shadow Boxing: Start in a defensive position (hands up and indicating you do not wish to fight) and imagine your attacker swings a wild punch at your head. Use the windup position as a flinch response to check and trap the arm **(Figure 25)**. Grab hold of his wrist or forearm with your back hand and pull in as you shuffle in with the cat stance (or as you pull backward into the back stance) and strike his neck with the lead forearm, ending in shuto uke position **(Figure 26)**. Strike a few more times, adding in palm heel strikes and/or elbows strikes, and then back away with your hands up in a defensive position. Switch your feet and repeat on the other side.

Figure 25

Figure 26

7. Shuto (Knife-Hand) Blocks with Lead Leg Front Kick

Traditional Kihon: Shuto (knife-hand) blocks in cat stance (or back stance) followed by a lead leg front kick, moving up and down the floor (**Figures 27-28**).

Figure 27

Figure 28

Practical Application Shadow Boxing: Imagine the fight has gotten away from you, and you shoot both hands forward to check a wild punch (augmented windup for the shuto block). Grasp the arm with one hand and strike the neck or side of the head with the other forearm, ending in shuto block position (**Figure 29**). Hook your hand around the back of his neck and pull him into a lead-leg front kick to the knee of his back leg (kicking out his leg to help take him down) or a knee strike to the groin or stomach (**Figure 30**). Deliver several kicks or knee strikes, add in some elbow strikes, and then back away with your hands up in a defensive position. Switch your feet and repeat on the other side.

Figure 29   *Figure 30*

Conclusion

In my own kihon training, I enjoy visualizing practical techniques while practicing the traditional movements. However, I find it much more beneficial to pair my traditional kihon practice with practical application shadow boxing. Sometimes, I don't have time for a long solo training session, and so I will do one or the other, depending upon what I feel I need more work on at that time in my training. (For example, if I'm trying to sharpen my kata performance, then I will do traditional kihon training, but if I'm working bunkai for my kata, then I will do practical application shadow boxing to put my body and brain in a bunkai frame of mind.) Either way, when you start training kihon in this way, you will quickly realize just how applicable traditional kihon training is for practical self-defense.

The Author with Iain Abernethy, 2017

4 KATA TRAINING AND BUNKAI

Why Kata?

Many martial arts systems and styles have some form of pre-arranged set of movements to aid the practice of that art. In karate, these forms are called kata, and kata is the very heart of karate. Even though kata practice is the foundation of all karate systems, no standard definition or singular understanding of kata exists. Shoshin Nagamine offers a concise and constructive definition: "Kata can be described as a systematically organized series of defensive and offensive techniques performed in a sequence against one or more imaginary opponents, and given a symmetrical, linear pattern."[1]

However, because the transference of kata, their meaning, and their performance have relied mainly on oral tradition from generation to generation, Nagamine concludes, "the manner in which kata should be executed is also open to various interpretations."[2] Of course, everyone has his/her own opinions about what is the best way to view, perform, and practice kata. In this chapter, I will outline some of my own views and offer specific suggestions to make your solo practice of kata as productive and engaging as possible.

Even if you don't practice kata or forms per se, you are likely to have some sets of drills or combined movements and techniques that you practice repetitively. One problem with such repetitive practice, be it with kata or other drills, is that many of us quickly tire of the repetition and become bored with the practice. In *Karate-Do Kyohan* Gichin Funakoshi explains that karate training takes years of practice and that we cannot expect to see good results quickly.

---

[1] Nagamine, *The Essence of Okinawan Karate-Do*, p. 55.
[2] *Ibid.*, p. 56.

Because any type of martial arts training requires a long-term commitment, there is the risk of burning out: "Many people become weary after training half a year or a year. This state of weariness, which is common and is not restricted to the study of karate, is a critical one, and a student may succeed or fail depending on his attitude during this period."[3] One way to overcome kata-training burnout—or weariness that accompanies any repetitive physical training—is to vary the training regimen. Below, I offer a variety of strategies for keeping your kata training fresh.

Figure 1: Kata Kusanku

Why practice kata? Mainly, kata or martial arts forms are classic training tools handed down to us from great masters, acting like a curriculum syllabus or a concise book of information expressing key combative principles illustrated by various techniques. The medium for combative information storage and transfer is the human body learning, practicing, and performing the kata. Repeated kata practice trains us in these core combative principles and fighting techniques.

---

[3] Funakoshi, *Karate-Do Kyohan*, p. 37.

The kata also teach us how to move in time and space while executing self-defense techniques against our imagined attacker. In an actual violent confrontation, you do not want to be standing still. Rather, you want to be moving constantly, taking the attack to the enemy, adopting an advantageous position while putting your attacker in disadvantaged position, and seeking opportunities to escape to safety. Kata practice properly understood and executed trains us in these types of combative movement dynamics.

Intense kata practice also develops our cardiovascular health, preparing us for actual civilian combat, which is fast, explosive, punishing, and exhausting. Real fights are nothing like the movies—they usually last several seconds only (that feel like minutes or even hours), and they leave you completely fatigued. Moreover, during a violent confrontation your body will be filled with adrenaline and other hormones, which affect your mind, behavior, emotions, and physical movement in a variety of ways.

Fighting in the dojo or the gym is totally different than fighting for your life in a self-defense situation. Practicing kata intensely, to complete exhaustion, and then continuing to practice through the exhaustion helps train you to cope with the harsh realities of an actual confrontation, should your attempts to be aware of danger, avoid problems, de-escalate encounters, and escape violence all fail, requiring that you fight your way out of the situation.

Figure 2: Kata Ananku

Figure 3: Kata Ananku

Finally, kata training helps refine our technique, form, movement, balance, and martial arts aesthetics. People train in the martial arts for many different reasons: health, exercise, enjoyment, artistic expression, competition, and self-defense. Some focus on one or a few of these contexts, while others may engage each of them to varying degrees throughout their lives of training. Because technique, form, movement, balance, and aesthetics are fundamental elements to each of these contexts, kata practice applies to all types of martial arts training.

Even if your martial arts system does not include kata or forms or if your dojo does not emphasize frequent kata practice, I hope you at least have a better understanding of why kata are so important, especially if approached with the proper understanding and training intent. Kata or forms are one of the best solo training tools, and they have been part of martial arts training for as far back as we have historical martial arts documentation.

WHAT IS BUNKAI?

When Anko Itosu introduced karate into the Okinawan schools in the early twentieth century, the teaching and training emphasis shifted from civilian combat to physical fitness, character building, and martial arts competition. Indeed, there is nothing inherently wrong with training in karate for health and sport; however, this type of training is not sufficient for developing self-defense and civilian combative skills. One major element lost in this transition to sport karate is bunkai training or the practical analysis and application of kata techniques. According to Jerry Figgiani, kata is the heart of karate, and bunkai is the heart of kata:

> The katas are the templates for the practitioner to understand the self-defense techniques that are hidden within these forms. I feel this is a very important part of the study of karate. To just do the physical movements of the kata without understanding the movement is an injustice to the practitioner. To understand the art is to dig deep into the kata for its hidden meanings. Working bunkai and understanding its principles help bring the kata to life.[4]

In other words, studying bunkai is fundamental to understanding karate specifically and the martial arts generally.

In centuries past, bunkai applications were practiced as partner drills and then organized into pre-arranged movements (the kata or forms) that could be practiced by oneself. As Patrick McCarthy explains, this method of training stems from classical Chinese kung fu as illustrated in the *Bubishi*. Essentially,

---

[4] Fraguas, *Karate Masters*, p. 23.

kung fu students were taught specific responses to certain types of attacks. Then, these responses where practiced in partner drills. Next, these responses were practiced solo for individual training, and then several movements were linked together into choreographed routines to be practiced solo and transmitted to others.[5] Eventually, such routines became the kata of karate, and each traditional kata expressed key self-defense combative principles of the master who created the kata. By studying the movements within the kata, practitioners learned specific types of self-defense responses to various attacks. The key to kata, according to Chris Clarke, is the bunkai expressed through them.[6]

As Iain Abernethy observes, many modern dojos teach kata because it is "traditional," because they are part of the curriculum, or for competition. The average practitioner may not really know why they are practicing kata, and they do so half-heartedly or even begrudgingly.[7] To study, train, and practice traditional karate is to dig deep into the kata, to learn their movements, and to analyze the application of these movements to civil combat and self-defense. In recent decades, many dojos have been returning to this more ancient tradition, and, ironically, taking karate into the future by returning to its past.

Figure 4: Neck crank bunkai from kata Pinan Godan

Figure 5: Neck strike bunkai from kata Wankan

Of course, bunkai study must involve partner training; however, we can still explore, discover, experiment with, develop, and practice bunkai techniques and concepts in our solo training. Let me be clear: I am NOT saying that solo

---

[5] McCarthy, *Bubishi*, pp. 18-19.
[6] Clarke, *American Shorin-Ryu Karate Association*, pp. 75-77.
[7] Abernethy, *Bunkai Jutsu*, Ch. 2.

bunkai training is sufficient, and I am NOT suggesting that solo bunkai practice can replace partner training. I AM saying, quite simply, that we can augment and supplement our bunkai training through creative solo practice that enlivens our kata practice.

Ways to Practice Kata and Solo Train Bunkai

Regardless of what you may have heard or learned, there is no one right way to practice your kata or forms. Sure, your sensei or instructor may have preferred methods, and you should always follow the instruction you receive when practicing in the dojo. However, when you are practicing on your own, you can experiment with other ways of training so as to enhance your learning and stem the tide of weariness that comes with any type of repetitive training. Below are some strategies I use to vary my kata and solo bunkai training. Give them a try. Keep what works for you, modify others to make them more applicable to your interests and training needs, and use them as creative inspiration for creating your own solo-training routines.

Kata and Bunkai Circuit Training

1. Warm up with a one-minute round of light shadow boxing with punches and elbow strikes, one minute of knee strikes and kicks, and one minute of punches, knees, and kicks.
2. Perform a kata at full speed and power.
3. One-minute round of shadow boxing a bunkai sequence from the kata, working the left lead and the right lead.
4. Perform a different kata at full speed and power.
5. One-minute round of shadow boxing a bunkai sequence from that kata, working the left and the right lead.
6. Continue until you get through all your kata or reach the time limit for that training session.

Note: Whenever you return to this training drill, try your best to shadow box different bunkai sequences from each of the kata. Or, instead of working different kata during a training session, consider focusing on one kata, concentrating your training on exploring the kata in depth.

Figure 6: Opening move of kata Pinan Yondan

Figure 7: Shadow boxing a headlock defense for the opening moves of kata Pinan Yondan

Alternating Speeds

1. Perform a kata in slow motion, focusing on technique, form, stances, angles, and body positioning.
2. Perform the same kata at medium speed and power, focusing on the self-corrections you made during the slow motion round.
3. Perform the kata at full speed and power, trying to maintain good form, technique, timing, breathing, angles, stances, and body positioning.

Note: You can do this with one kata for the whole session, or work on a few kata in this manner.

Bunkai Visualization

- Perform a kata at varying speeds, each time visualizing the practical bunkai moves of each key sequence.
- Try to keep the visualizations practical, remembering that "blocks" are not always blocks (e.g., the high block can be a forearm thrust to the throat), and punches are not always punches (e.g., a high punch could actually be a neck crank in which the punching hand is thrusting the attacker's chin and the hikite hand is pulling the back of the head/hair, thus twisting the head and neck).

Bunkai Kata

Some karate practitioners may find this next training strategy extremely controversial, but have an open mind and give it a try. Please note that I revere the original form of all kata, and you should always perform the kata according to the power dynamics and stylistic dictates of your martial arts system. Again, I am NOT advocating changing the kata itself. However, we can bridge the gap between the (sometimes) artificial look and feel of a kata and practical application by training "bunkai kata."

- Imagine you are defending yourself against an attacker roughly your same size or a bit larger, and perform the kata movements *as if you are fighting for your life*, using the practical applications associated with each movement and sequence of techniques.
- Your hand positions may not be exactly as in the kata (for example, if that "high block" is a strike to the throat, it won't end in the normal "high block" position), your stances may not be exactly the same each time, depending upon your application or use of that stance in various portions of the kata, your angles may not be exactly as in the kata (as those angles are the ideal), and your *embusen* (the spot where a kata begins and ends) will most likely be off. Don't worry—you are performing practical self-defense movements in solo practice, not the aesthetic kata.

For some traditional martial artists, this drill may seem like heresy. Please forgive me if that is your reaction. However, I encourage you to have an open mind and to differentiate between the stylized kata and the application of its techniques. This drill seeks to bridge the gap between the aesthetic kata and the "uglier" practical application of the movements.

Again, I am NOT advocating changing the kata. This drill is not intended to replace regular, traditional kata practice. Rather, this strategy enhances and supplements kata practice, seeking to bridge the distance between aesthetics and application.

Figure 8: Fukyugata I first move traditional form—high block

Figure 9: Fukyugata I second move traditional form—step punch

Figure 10: Fukyugata I third move traditional form—step back low block

Figure 11: Fukyugata I first move bunkai form—lapel grab defense striking the neck or throat

Figure 12: Fukyugata I second move bunkai form—pulling the grabbing arm at crook of elbow to twist enemy's body and punch to head

Figure 13: Fukyugata I third move bunkai form—retaining hold of his grasping hand, stepping back, and striking low to groin

Bunkai Counting

- When breaking a kata down, we often count numerically before each sequence.
- Instead of counting, try calling out a bunkai application before executing the movement in the kata.
- For example, the first movement of Matusbayashi-ryu's Fukyugata Ich (the first basic kata/form in the system) is to turn 90 degrees to the left and execute a low block in front stance, then step forward with the right

foot into walking stance and punch at chest level. Instead of counting *ich* (or one), call out a bunkai application (pulling the attacker's lead hand down while getting to his outside, then pulling that hand in while stepping and punching) and execute that portion of the kata.
- You'll find this strategy to be an effective and efficient way to practice kata as well as reviewing and remembering the practical bunkai.

Bunkai Breakdown

1. Divide a kata into practical bunkai sequences.
2. Practice each sequence portion five times in a row, refining and correcting your movements and techniques.
3. After all the key sequences have been practiced five times each, perform the kata straight through at full speed and power.
4. Notice how in your mind the kata flows yet you are more aware of the practical bunkai sequencing within the full kata.

Concentrated Kata and Bunkai Session

1. Choose one kata for a 30-minute session
2. Perform the kata slowly and then medium pace a few times as a warm up.
3. Perform the kata full speed and power.
4. Next, shadow box bunkai applications from the first main portion of the kata, three times on both sides (left lead and right lead).
5. Then perform the kata at full speed and power.
6. Shadow box bunkai applications from the next main portion of the kata, three times on both sides.
7. Back to performing the whole kata at full speed and power.
8. Work your way through the whole kata, shadow boxing bunkai applications for each main portion. By the end, you'll discover a whole new appreciation for that kata and a deeper understanding of its practical applications.

Figure 14: Pinan Shodan first move traditional form—high block, chest block

Figure 15: Pinan Shodan second move traditional form—inside chest block

Figure 16: Pinan Shodan third move traditional form—punch

Figure 17: Pinan Shodan first move shadow box bunkai—flinch response

Figure 18: Pinan Shodan second move shadow box bunkai—hammer fist to side of head

Figure 19: Pinan Shodan third move shadow box bunkai—control limb and punch head

Sequence Repetition

1. Perform the kata straight through.
2. Divide the kata into sequences, either by traditional count (as per your style's conventions) or by your own bunkai sections.
3. Perform the first sequence three times.
4. At the end of the third repetition, perform the next sequence three times.
5. At the end of the third repetition of that sequence, perform the next sequence three times.
6. Continue until you finish the kata.

Note: Each repetition can be at the same speed and intensity, or you can perform the first at slow motion, the second medium speed and power, and the third at full speed and power.

Look! No Hands!

- Choose a kata and practice the foot work or lower body portions only, keeping your hands in a fighting guard or on your hips.
- Concentrate your attention and correction on stances, transitions between stances, body positioning, and correct angles.
- You can also carry weights in both hands as you perform the lower body parts of the kata to make it a strengthening exercise.

Phone Booth Kata

- Choose a kata and practice the hand techniques only, shifting your feet into the next stance and direction but without actually moving.
- This exercise is great for practicing kata in a confined space, like an office (for those quick lunch-break practice sessions), hotel room, or living room (why not review kata while watching TV?).
- Concentrate your attention and correction on your hand positions, power, form, technique, and form of your stances.
- You can also hold small hand weights or wear wrist weights to make it a strengthening exercise.

Kata as Strength Builders

- Practice the kata and bunkai applications while wearing ankle and wrist weights.
- Start with light weights, and perform the kata at a slow pace at first, gradually building up to medium pace.
- After a few repetitions, remove the weights and perform the kata at full speed and power and notice the difference. You should feel like the Flash, zipping through the kata!

- Be especially careful if you have any joint or muscle injuries, as this type of training may worsen the injury or reinjure a recently healed muscle or joint.

Kicking and Screaming

- Try to *kiai* (yell) on each technique, not just in the customary ones.
- Notice the difference in your power and intensity—the kata should really feel and look deadly!

Exponential Kata

1. Perform the first move of a kata and return to the beginning.
2. Perform the next two moves and return to the beginning.
3. Then, perform the next three moves, and back to the beginning.
4. Continue in this manner until you build up to all of the movements in the kata.
5. You should be sufficiently exhausted! Perform the kata one more time straight through with all the speed and power you can muster.

Note: You can practice this drill at varying speeds and levels of intensity. This drill encourages focused repetition and concentrated study of each movement while building them in sequence. You'll never view that kata the same way again!

Multidirectional Practice

- Practice a kata eight times, each repetition facing a different one of the eight direction points.
- In other words, face a direction and perform the kata. Then, rotate 45 degrees to the right and perform the kata again. Then, rotate another 45 degrees and perform the kata again. Repeat until you are facing the first direction again.
- Multidirectional kata practice helps us overcome our subconscious reliance on visual spatial cues when learning and practicing kata.

Blind Kata

- Practice your kata with your eyes closed.
- Make sure there are no obstructions in your practice area, and make sure you are far enough away from walls, furniture, and other objects.
- Practice a few times in slow motion and then gradually build up your speed and power as you become more comfortable training with your eyes closed.
- Use a blindfold if you find yourself peaking too much.
- Blind kata practice helps us focus on our own body and its movement through time and space based upon feeling and proprioception (our innate ability to sense our body's position in space).

Blind Multidirectional Practice

- Perform the kata at each of the eight points of direction, but keep your eyes closed (or wear a blindfold).
- Be sure to keep your eyes closed (or the blindfold on) throughout all eight repetitions. Do not open your eyes between each kata performance. How close do you end up at the starting point when you are finished?
- This drill develops and hones our combative proprioception.

Reverse Kata

- So, you think you really know your kata? Practice one in reverse!
- Start from the last movement and work your way to the first movement. It's much harder than you think.
- This drill mainly tests how well you know the moves and their sequences, and I don't think there are any good benefits of this drill for practical bunkai training (however, I could be wrong on this point).

  Full disclosure: I'm terrible at this exercise!

Reverse Blind Kata

- If you really want to get crazy, perform a kata backwards while blindfolded.
- Enough said…

Everyday Kata

- Conduct a kata and solo bunkai practice session in your street clothes, or your normal work clothes, including footwear.
- If you are a traditional martial artist, you probably train in some kind of gi or uniform as per your style and system. However, you will not likely be attacked in the street while wearing a gi. So, it's a good idea to practice your techniques and applications in normal clothing.

Figure 20: Opening move of kata Wanshu—fist in palm with knee raised

Figure 21: Shadow boxing bunkai for opening move of kata Wanshu—neck crank and knee strike to ribs or back

Multiple Locations

- Change up the location of your kata practice:
    - Nice dojo or gym space.
    - Your living room or other small space (office, hotel room, small garage)—practice the upper-body movements while shifting your feet and stances without moving around too much.
    - In a park.
    - On the beach.

- In knee- or waist-deep water.
- Underwater!
- On the side of a short hill.
- On a gravel driveway.
- In the woods.
- On an icy patch or ice skating rink (be extremely careful!).
- Changing our training locations allows us to consider how much we take stable footing in the dojo for granted. How effective are those high kicks and spinning techniques on gravel or ice?

Figure 22: Kata Wankan front kicks going uphill

Figure 23: Kata Kusanku front kick on gravel drive

Video Kata

- Video record your kata (most everyone has a smartphone with video camera these days) and then review it. You will see much more to work on than you might have expected.
- You can also video yourself performing the same kata 10 or 20 times at full speed. Notice how your techniques and stances change as you become more fatigued.
- Also, consider sharing the videos with your sensei for more instruction, especially if you are truly ronin and live far away from your sensei and have not yet found a new sensei with whom to train.

Sequential Kata Practice

- Practice your kata from the basic to the most advanced, performing each

one at full speed and power, and taking only a five-second break between each kata.
- Note how difficult it is to perform the more intricate techniques in the advanced kata while fatigued.
- This drill enables us to practice techniques under great fatigue and with adrenaline in our system, thus helping us condition ourselves for civilian combat.

Reverse Sequential Kata Practice

- Practice your kata from the most advanced to the basic, performing each one at full speed and power, taking only a five-second break between each kata.
- Note how difficult it is to perform the basic techniques of the simple kata while fatigued. Also, note how often you make mistakes in each of the kata, especially the more advanced ones, because you are performing them out of their normal sequence!
- Similarly, this drill enables us to practice techniques under great fatigue and a bit of disorientation (performing the kata out of sequence), as well as with adrenaline in our system, thus helping us condition ourselves for civilian combat.

CONCLUSION

Repetitive kata practice may seem rather dull. Let's be honest, for most of us in the modern world of immediate technological gratification, constant social media access, and endless shows and movies on Netflix and Amazon Prime, kata repetition can easily bore us. However, if we want to excel in our martial arts training, then we must practice our kata, forms, and other solo drills over and over again.

Practice may not make perfect, but repeated practice will build proficiency. To make the repetition more fun and to ward off becoming weary of practice, try some of the suggestions described above. Also, tap into your innate creativity and develop your own tips and tricks for making kata and solo bunkai practice fun, efficient, and efficacious.

Author kneeing a heavy bag

5 IMPACT TRAINING

IMPORTANCE OF HITTING STUFF

Many modern martial artists, such as MMA and Krav Maga practitioners, who watch traditional martial artists punching and kicking the air while marching up and down the training floor sometimes scoff dismissively: "What good is striking the air? You need to hit stuff to test your strikes and to toughen your limbs so that they won't buckle or break in an actual confrontation!" They are absolutely correct! Martial artists definitely need impact training.

However, those who dismiss the traditional martial arts as hopelessly impractical and outdated are woefully incorrect in their assessment. Indeed, there are some martial arts schools claiming to be traditional that do not ask their students to actually hit stuff. But, such schools do not fully represent true traditional martial arts, because impact training has always been an essential component of martial arts training.

Whether we like it or not, there truly is nothing new under the sun. All the fancy bag work we see in boxing, MMA, Krav Maga, and other modern martial arts is really nothing new. Sure, some of the strategies, routines, and equipment may be new, but the principles of impact training are as old as the martials arts themselves.

For example, ancient Chinese martial arts, which heavily influenced the various Asian fighting systems, employed a variety of impact training strategies to strengthen the body and prepare the limbs for combat. Chinese impact training implements included bamboo poles, wooden dummies (complete with torso, head and limbs), clay tiles, wooden boards, and bags (filled with rice, grain, sand, dirt, or stones) affixed to tables or swinging from ropes.[1]

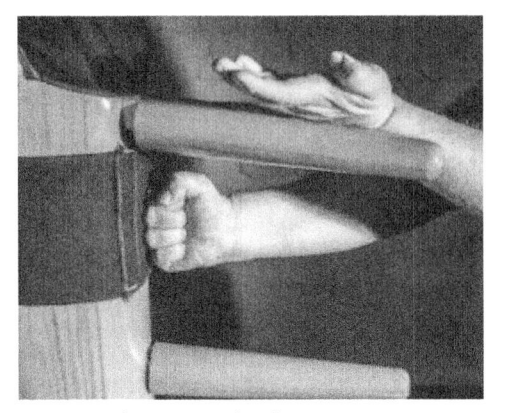

Figure 1: Chinese wooden dummy
Source: Shutterstock

Figure 2: Chinese clay tiles
Source: Shutterstock

In karate, the *makiwara* is an ancient impact training implement still used today in dojos throughout the world. In "Ten Lessons of To-te," Anko Itosu stated, "One of the most important issues in karate is the importance of training the hands and feet. Therefore, one must always make use of the *makiwara* in order to develop them thoroughly."[2] Impact training on the *makiwara* is so important to true traditional karate, that Choki Motobu devotes an entire chapter in his book *Okinawan Kempo* on how to make and train with the *makiwara*.[3]

Similarly, Gichin Funakoshi includes an appendix in his book *Karate-Do Kyohan* on how to make and use a standing and hanging *makiwara*,[4] and he explains in *Karate-Do Nyumon* that *makiwara* training is important to strengthening the hands and feet to withstand actual combative striking.[5] Finally, when discussing *atemi* (the powerful strikes found in karate), Shoshin Nagamine argues that the student of karate must strengthen and harden the hands and feet by practicing on a *makiwara*, and he briefly describes the basic dimensions and composition of a traditional *makiwara*.[6]

---

[1] Kennedy and Guo, *Chinese Martial Arts Training Manuals*, pp. 17-26.
[2] Quoted in Nagamine, *Tales of Okinawa's Great Masters*, p. 57.
[3] Motobu, *Okinwan Kempo*, pp. 41-51.
[4] Funakoshi, *Karate-Do Kyohan* pp. 251-52.
[5] Funakoshi, *Karate-Do Nyumon*, pp. 52-53.
[6] Nagamine, *The Essence of Okinawan Karate-Do*, pp. 249-50.

Figure 3: Okinawan makiwara

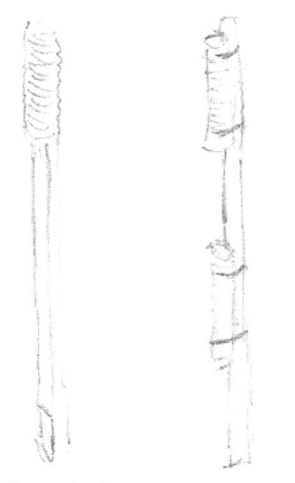

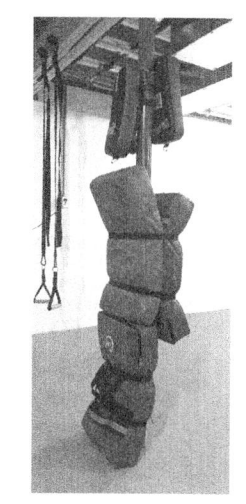

Figure 4: Simulated makiwara

Impact training is essential to all martial arts, and it should be a significant component of any solo training regimen. As the ancients well knew, practitioners must do more than merely punch and kick the air. We must strike stuff. Only by hitting and kicking a heavy bag or some impact training device can we develop strong techniques. We must experience the physical feedback from punching and kicking a solid object. We must also condition our limbs and strengthen our joints to withstand the force and pressure dynamics associated with striking an opponent.

Indeed, various types of partner training can aid in this conditioning (particularly partner pad work), but for obvious safety and health reasons, we cannot constantly wail on our training partners during sparring, and we won't always have a partner handy to hold pads and target mitts. Thus, solo impact training must be integrated into our martial arts practice. Repeated impact training will provide the necessary conditioning to enable us to execute effective and devastating strikes in a self-defense situation.

However, be sure to consult your family doctor before engaging in any intense form of impact training. Just because your sensei, instructor, or training partner can wail on a heavy bag or *makiwara* for hours on end doesn't mean you can also. Make sure your body is capable of enduring such training. Also, if you are new to impact training, start slow and gradually increase repetition and intensity.

I once heard a senior instructor in one of the first karate organizations I joined back in the late 1980s tell the following story of his own impact training. He took a phone book and placed it on a wooden chair. Every day, he would tear out one page and then punch downward on the book 100 times. A year or so later, when he ran out of pages in the phone book, he was able to hit the hard wood chair at full force and not hurt his hand. I'm not suggesting we all do this, but his example illustrates the main idea: increase the intensity gradually over time so as to condition your limbs and strengthen the joints.

One last issue to consider: to wear protective hand and feet gear or not. Different people have different views on this question, and you must decide for yourself. The senior sensei I mentioned above did not use protective hand gear when hitting the chair and when punching and kicking the *makiwara*. As a result, he had hands and feet like stone—and they looked like stone as well. The knuckles on his hands and feet were calloused, swollen, disfigured, and aesthetically displeasing. Sure, when he punched or kicked you, it hurt like hell! But his hands and feet were ugly, troll ugly. He didn't care; nor did his wife. Great! More power to him.

Such conditioning of your hands and feet will produce incredibly strong striking weapons, but in addition to making them terribly unattractive (which may not concern you), such conditioning also greatly increases the risk of arthritis and other such debilitating joint and bone conditions. If you don't want to damage your hands and feet permanently, then consider using such protective gear as sparring gear, heavy bag gloves, or hand and wrist wraps when impact training. There are benefits and drawbacks to both choices, and only you can decide what is best for you, your training, and the ultimate goals of your martial arts practice.

Figure 5: Hand wraps

Figure 6: Heavy bag gloves

CLASSICAL KARATE *MAKIWARA* TRAINING

If you are not training in a traditional karate style or system, then *makiwara* practice may not be for you. However, if you are open to trying new things, or if you are a traditional karate practitioner, then you should consider integrating *makiwara* practice into your solo impact training routines. Hardcore karate traditionalists insist on making their own *makiwara*. If DIY is your thing, then by all means give it a go. You can search the Internet and find several excellent sets of instructions for designing and mounting your own *makiwara*. However, do yourself a favor and conduct some extensive research. Don't go with the first Google search result. Find and compare several sets of instructions, and use your common sense. Follow the instructions that seem most reasonable, informed, and safe to you.

Consider creating both the hanging type (*age-makiwara*) and the stationary type (*tachi-makiwara*). The *age-makiwara* is excellent for developing footwork and hand speed along with conditioning your hands. If you create a *tachi-makiwara* consider including both the punching target and a knee-level kicking target, thus allowing you to condition your fists and your feet (traditional Okinawan karate kicks are generally knee, thigh, and groin level, as that is most effective and practical for self-defense). If you are not much of a DIY person, then consider purchasing *makiwara* kits online through such sites as Makiwarakarate.com, AWMA.com, or Amazon.com.

When training on the *age-makiwara* (the hanging style), be sure to integrate footwork along with your punching and kicking (you can hang the target at various heights for punching and kicking). Practice shuffle steps, moving toward and away from the target, shifting from side to side, working angles of attack, bobbing and weaving, and ducking techniques. In addition to hand and foot conditioning, the *age-makiwara* helps you develop leg and torso strength, improve timing, gauge distance, and enhance your footwork in conjunction with your striking and kicking.

Tachi-makiwara training mainly develops punching and kicking strength and conditions your hands, feet, and respective joints (wrists, elbows, shoulders, ankles, knees, and hips). Traditionally, karateka practice lunge punches, reverse punches, front kicks, round house kicks (striking with the ball of the foot), and side kicks on the *makiwara*. However, you can be creative and also train your traditional blocks as strikes (as they were originally intended, in my opinion): knife-hand blocks, inside and outside chest blocks, and low blocks, as well as elbow and knee strikes.

Basic Heavy Bag Work

If punching wood poles wrapped with rope is not quite your training cup of tea, then consider working out on a heavy bag. Most gyms and dojos have heavy bags, so make use of them for solo training when possible. If you have a workout room, home gym, or available space in your garage or basement, consider purchasing your own heavy bag for personal training anytime. Consider a six-foot heavy bag that hangs close to the floor, so that you can work leg-level strikes and knee strikes more effectively.

Be careful to suspend the heavy bag properly so as not to damage the structural integrity of your ceiling. The bags are indeed heavy, and repeated impact from punching and kicking puts significant stress on the joists and cross beams. If hanging from the ceiling is not an option, you can purchase a heavy bag stand. Be sure to properly anchor your stand with sufficient weights to keep it from sliding around or tipping over.

Another excellent heavy bag option is the basic wave bag—a heavy bag with a weighted base that can be filled with water or sand. In addition to working a heavy bag, try bashing a Bob punching dummy. They are quite fun to strike, and you can work your accuracy and striking surfaces more carefully than a heavy bag. Of course, Bob punching dummies are more expensive, but if you can train on one, do it!

Training on a heavy bag is limited only by your imagination. Whatever your martial arts level, from absolute beginner to seasoned advanced student, you can develop your own unique training sessions. Review all of your striking techniques (closed-hand strikes, open-hand strikes, elbows, knees, various kicks, shin kicks, shoulder bumps, bicep bumps, forearm strikes), and then create circuit training sessions that work them all in various orders. Some days you can review the tried and true techniques, while other days you can practice the techniques you most recently learned.

If you are creative and a little daring, you can also work some basic throws and grappling moves on a six-foot heavy bag. Replace the chains with rope, or remove the chains and tie old martial arts belts tightly around the top section of the bag to simulate arms. Then, grasp the ropes or belt ends and "shoot in" to practice various types of throws, like the hip toss, winding throw, neck throw, or reaping throw. However, be especially careful if you have any back problems, working the techniques at slow to moderate speeds. Lay the bag on the ground, and you can practice moving into and out of various guards and mounted positions, executing punches, elbow strikes, and knee strikes.

The following is a basic heavy bag workout routine. Be creative and develop your own that suits your martial arts style and training needs. You can do sets of various techniques, performing a specific number of repetitions within each set and working both sides of your body by switching your lead leg. Or, consider using an interval timer app on your smartphone, preferably one that also plays music during the intervals, and create a circuit routine with several one-minute rounds, each separated by a ten-to-fifteen-second round. Be sure to warm up adequately first and include some ballistic stretching before starting your heavy bag workout.

1. Minute of left jabs
2. 15 seconds of rest (or pushups)
3. Minute of right jabs
4. 15 seconds of rest (or sit ups)
5. Minute of left-lead jab-cross combinations
6. 15 seconds of rest (or pushups including pulling the hand back into hikite position or the side of your body between pushups)
7. Minute of right-lead jab-cross combinations
8. 15 seconds of rest (or leg lifts)
9. Minute of front kicks, alternating feet
10. 15 seconds of rest (or pushups including reaching up to the ceiling between pushups)
11. Minute of jab-cross-front kick combinations, alternating feet
12. 15 seconds of rest (or right-side plank)
13. Minute of round-house kicks, alternating feet
14. 15 seconds of rest (or pushups positioning the hands out wide)
15. Minute of jab-cross-round-house-kick combinations, alternating feet
16. 15 seconds of rest (or left-side plank)
17. Minute of side kicks, alternating feet
18. 15 seconds of rest (or squats)
19. Minute of jab-cross-side-kick combinations, alternating feet
20. 15 seconds of rest (or pushups with hands positioned close together)
21. Minute of jab-cross-hook combinations, alternating feet
22. 15 seconds of rest (or squat jumps)
23. Minute of elbow strikes (two-three strikes in a row), alternating feet
24. 15 seconds of rest (or jumping jacks)
25. Minute of knee strikes (two-three strikes in a row), alternating feet
26. 15 seconds of rest (or spotty dogs)
27. Minute of elbow and knee strike combinations, alternating feet

28. 15 seconds of rest (or light jogging in place)

This basic routine is about 17.5 minutes long, incorporating all the basic fighting techniques found in nearly all martial arts systems. And, it's a killer workout, depending upon how hard you work each minute round and if you rest or throw in the short strengthening exercises between each minute round. Of course, you can add other techniques or switch some out to suit your own training interests and needs.

BUNKAI IMPACT TRAINING

As discussed in the previous chapter on kata and bunkai training, bunkai simply means analyzing your kata or forms and pulling out practical self-defense applications and combative principles. Clearly, all practical martial arts training must—I repeat, must—involve various types of partner training, ranging from compliant and slow to non-compliant and aggressive. We must practice our practical self-defense bunkai techniques with training partners. However, we can enhance partner training with solo bunkai training, through kata and bunkai solo practice as described in the previous chapter, and through solo bunkai impact training.

In addition to wailing on the heavy bag or the Bob dummy with traditional punches, strikes, and kicks, we can also use impact training to practice our practical bunkai and to develop speed and power in our self-defense techniques. No matter how hard we may train with a partner, we still must hold back. We simply cannot go full on, blasting our partners in the face, throat, neck, groin, elbow joints, and knee joints with all the speed and power we can muster. We will run out of training partners, senseis, teachers, and friends pretty quickly. (Not to mention going broke from lawsuits.) So, supplement your partner bunkai and self-defense training with creative impact training.

If your martial arts system does not have kata or forms, then identify the major self-defense techniques and combative principles that you have been taught and that you practice with partners during a normal class session. Consider how you might work those techniques on a heavy bag. Some systems have one-steps, or combination drills, or kempo drills in which one person initiates a particular kind of attack, and the other person executes a defense and counter (or, ideally, a response that consolidates the defense and counter into a seamless and simple movement, followed up by a series of counter strikes to facilitate escape). Figure out ways to practice these combination sets on a heavy bag or a Bob dummy.

If you come from a traditional system with kata or forms, then pull out the major practical bunkai techniques from your kata and impact train them. Now, a quick word about bunkai versus practical bunkai. There are many traditional martial arts systems that drill bunkai techniques, but they may not be practical. Such systems have drills in which the attacker starts in a low-block position in front stance while the defender stands in ready position, usually with hands positioned in front of the belt. Then, the attacker steps in and lunge punches, holding the arm out, as the defender executes a block and counter from the kata or form. Or, the defender stands in the middle of several people and performs the kata or form as the other people step in with traditional karate lunge-punch attacks.

However valuable these exercises may be for martial arts training, this is not the kind of bunkai I am talking about. Such bunkai are not practical. How many people are standing still in the street while the mugger gets into a low-block, forward-stance position, screams, and then lunges in with a single punch to the chest or chin? Never. Never, ever. Never, ever, never. Please, hear me: I mean no offense here. However, this kind of "bunkai practice" is not true bunkai and is not traditional. Such practice is a modern invention based upon misunderstanding of bunkai.[7]

Practical bunkai are self-defense applications designed to work in actual civilian combat, in attacks on the street, and against real acts of violence people face in daily life. These acts of violence include such things as the following:

- sucker punches,
- blitz attacks,
- blindside rush attacks,
- aggressive gesturing or finger pointing accompanied by cursing and foul language as the attacker closes the gap to attack,
- clinch fighting,
- choking,
- hair grabbing,
- headlocks followed by punches to the head,
- bear hug takedowns (from the front, rear, and sides),
- bear hugs from behind used in abduction attempts,

---

[7] For an excellent introduction to and discussion of practical bunkai training, see Abernethy, *Bunkai Jutsu*.

- low tackles (from all angles),
- waist-level and shoulder-level tackles (from all angles),
- arm-bars and full nelsons (usually with the intent to hold you still while another attacker punches and kicks you either to unconsciousness or even death),
- other such horrifically terrifying assault strategies.

Traditional kata and forms were designed to protect against these types of attacks.[8] Learn to pull out the respective self-defense techniques found in your kata and forms, and practice them with partners, solo training (as described in Chapter 4), and solo impact training.

The following are a few examples of bunkai impact training drills using a basic standing heavy bag apparatus. In each description, I name the kata or form from which the techniques are derived, as found in the Matsubayashi-ryu karate system. Even if you do not know these kata/forms, you can still get a sense for what I'm describing, and you may recognize similar techniques or combinations from your own kata or combination drills you happen to practice. Whatever your martial system, identify various bunkai, self-defense, or kempo combinations and then figure out how to drill them solo using impact equipment. Note, you should work the techniques on both sides of your body (switching your lead leg), and you can either do sets (with ten repetitions on both sides, for example) or minute rounds.

High Blocks from Fukyugata Ich

In the middle of the kata, you execute a right high block in walking stance, pivot 90 degrees to the right and low block right in front stance, step up with the left foot and high block with the left hand in walking stance (**Figure 7**), then shift 45 degrees to the left with the left foot into left-lead walking stance (**Figure 8**), and reverse punch right (**Figure 9**).

---

[8] For further discussion of kata and habitual acts of physical violence, see McCarthy, *Bubishi*, pp. 17-19.

Figure 7  *Figure 8*  *Figure 9*

The high-block motion can be used as a defense against a lapel grab. Generally, a person has grabbed your lapel so as to control your movement, target you more easily, and punch you repeatedly in the head. A basic bunkai application of the high block defends against the lapel grab attack. Although this sequence explores two different approaches to dealing with a successful lapel grab, I will describe only one application here as an illustration of how to use impact training to supplement your bunkai or application training. Sometimes it is difficult to visualize the grabbing hand, but you can tie a belt around the heavy bag to simulate the attacker's limb. (See the section WORKING THE HIKITE at the end of this chapter.)

High Block Application Impact Training Drill:

1. Reach up and grab the person's gripping hand.
2. Strike the crook of his elbow with the windup motion to jolt his body forward and to expose his neck.
3. Thrust your forearm into his neck or throat, using the high block motion (**Figure 10**).
4. Reach back down, grasp the crook of his elbow, and pull it across your body, thus twisting his body and exposing his kidney and/or floating rib.
5. Using the reverse punch, strike his kidney and/or floating rib area (**Figure 11**).
6. Remember, kata only provides an example illustrating the combative principle, and you can (should!) add other techniques as appropriate. In this drill, I pull the head back and downward and knee strike to the back (**Figure 12**). You could follow the knee strike with elbow strikes with other hand (**Figure 13**).

7. Back away defensively and repeat on the other side.

Figure 10

Figure 11

Figure 12

Figure 13

Middle Section of Fukyugata Ni

In this portion of the kata, a chest block (**Figure 14**) is followed by a front snap kick (**Figure 15**), upper-cut elbow strike (**Figure 16**), low block (**Figure 17**), reverse punch (**Figure 18**), and then a shuto strike to the neck (**Figure 19**).

Figure 14    *Figure 15*    *Figure 16*

Figure 17    *Figure 18*    *Figure 19*

This sequence can be applied as a way to escape from a clinch scenario. From a basic clinch position, the initial chest block can be used as an inward forearm strike to the side of the neck or as an upper-cut punch to the throat or chin (each of which ends in a position that looks exactly like the chest-block position). This combination is a blast to practice on a heavy bag.

1. Upper-cut strike the bag (**Figure 20**), front kick knee level (or knee strike) with the other foot (**Figure 21**), and step forward. Imagine the enemy is now leaning forward a bit due to his leg being kicked back or being kneed in the groin.
2. Upper-cut elbow strike (to the head) with the same arm as the foot that is forward (**Figure 22**).

3. Hammer fist low to the groin (**Figure 23**). This is the low block motion, which can also be used to clear limbs. Then, reverse punch (**Figure 24**). The hikite or pulling hand can be controlling a limb.
4. Step back for distance and shuto strike at neck level (**Figure 25**), using the hikite or pulling hand to control a limb, keep the enemy from protecting his head, and pulling him into the strike.
5. Back away defensively and repeat on the other side.

Figure 20

Figure 21

Figure 22

Figure 23

Figure 24

Figure 25

Opening Sequence of Pinan Shodan (Heian Nidan)

The simultaneous chest-block and high-block motion to the side can be used as a counter-ambush technique against a variety of blitz attacks. **Figures 26-31** represent the opening six moves of kata Pinan Shodan.

Figure 26

Figure 27

Figure 28

Figure 29

Figure 30

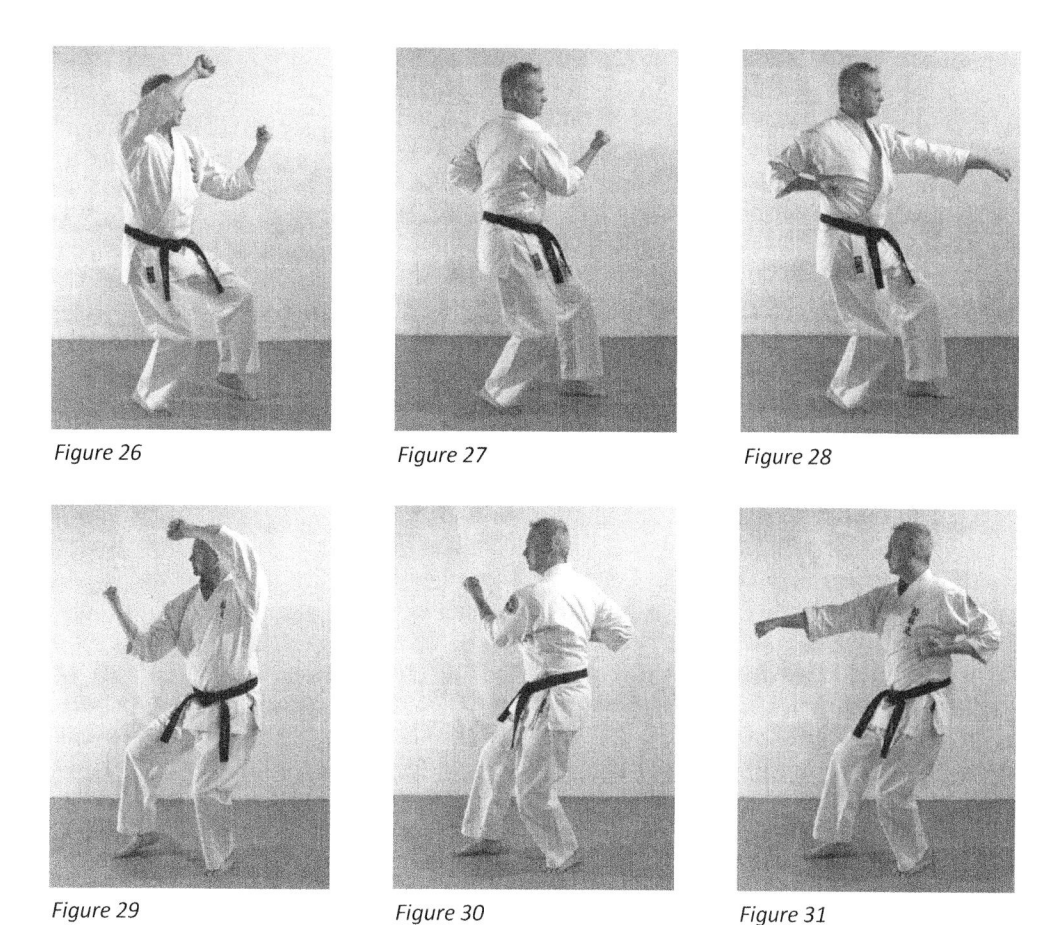

Figure 31

Counter-ambush techniques, like the opening sequence of Pinan Shodan, are quick flinch responses that can be used against various attacks. These techniques 1) place you in a more advantageous position as they put your attacker at a relative disadvantage, 2) inflict some damage upon your attacker, 3) protect you as they set you up for counter strikes, and 4) facilitate escape.

1. As the attack comes in, shift to the right or the left of the attacker, depending upon which side the attack comes from (the kata demonstrates the movement to both sides, indicating that you can shift to either side of the attacker and perform the same counters).
2. Your high-blocking arm can check his limb (a strike or an attempted grab), and the chest-blocking arm can be checking his other limb (in the case of an attempted high bear hug or tackle), jamming into his chest or

shoulder to create distance (**Figure 32**), or be an uppercut strike to the chin.
3. The kata then provides an example counter strike: hammer fist to the temple or side of the jaw (**Figure 33**), followed by a punch to any open target (**Figure 34**).
4. Back away defensively (**Figure 35**) and repeat on the other side.

Figure 32

Figure 33

Figure 34

Figure 35

Hammer Fist, Front Kick, Elbow Strike Combination in Pinan/Heian Yondan

This sequence starts with both hands being pulled to the side (**Figure 36**), followed by a simultaneous front snap kick (some styles use side kick) and hammer fist (**Figure 37**), followed by an elbow strike in cat stance (**Figure 38**).

Figure 36 *Figure 37* *Figure 38*

This bunkai application represents a defense against a successful lapel grab. Of course, we should try to prevent grabs as much as possible, but sometimes the enemy successfully grabs our garment as an attempt to control our movement and to target strikes more effectively.

1. Imagine your lapel has been grabbed. Reach up with same side hand and seize the grabbing hand as you cover with the other hand to protect from possible strikes (**Figure 39**).
2. Simultaneously, slap the side of the enemy's head with the other hand (**Figure 40**) and then seize the grabbing hand, such that both hands are seizing his hand on your lapel.
3. Rotate the hand over and pull to your opposite side, thus straightening the arm and bending the attacker over. Both of your hands are now at your side, as in the kata (**Figure 41**).
4. Use the front snap kick to kick out one of his legs, thus dropping him down on one knee (or at least leaning him over significantly), putting his head roughly at your shoulder level (**Figure 42**).
5. Hammer fist his head (**Figure 43**), reach around to the back of his head, grab his hair or cup his head, slide up, and elbow strike the side of his head (**Figure 44**).

6. Back away defensively and repeat on the other side.

Figure 39

Figure 40

Figure 41

Figure 42

Figure 43

Figure 44

Naihanchi/Tekki Shodan Opening Sequence

The Naihanchi kata are great fighting forms, emphasizing in-close, clinch-fighting combative principles. The opening sequence of Naihanchi/Tekki Shodan involves clinching, shovel kicks and/or knee strikes, leg sweeps, elbow strikes, and other brutal combative techniques. The kata performs these opening movements to the left and then to the right, indicating these techniques can be executed on either side, depending upon which side of the enemy you are on (**Figures 45-50**).

Figure 45    *Figure 46*    *Figure 47*

Figure 48    *Figure 49*    *Figure 50*

For this drill, I'm using the leg raise, outside knife-hand strike, elbow strike, low block, and hook or cross punch as a set of techniques for effectively dealing with a clinch-fighting scenario.

1. As you are clinched up, you can be throwing some knee strikes to the groin or shovel kicks to the knee (the leg raise at the beginning) as you reposition both hands behind his head. Grab around the back of the heavy bag and throw a few knee strikes (**Figure 51**).
2. Step off to the left, place your left hand on your left lapel (simulating grasping the enemy's hand that has grabbed your lapel) and strike at neck level with the outside of your right forearm, open hand, palm up (**Figure 52**).
3. With the right hand that was just striking, reach around to the back of the heavy bag (as if gripping his head) and elbow strike the bag with the left hand (**Figure 53**). You can strike multiple times. (The kata shows one

elbow strike as an example, but you can hit the enemy as many times as possible!)
4. With the arm that delivered the elbow strike(s), reach around the back of the bag, strike with the forearm, and simulate grabbing the enemy's face or chin (**Figure 54**).
5. Simulate pulling the enemy's head around and downward (the low block motion) (**Figure 55**), and deliver several hook punches to the bag with the other hand, simulating strikes to the enemy's head/neck (**Figure 56**).
6. Back away defensively and repeat on the other side.

Figure 51

Figure 52

Figure 53

Figure 54

Figure 55

Figure 56

Opening Moves of Ananku

Kata Ananku is an explosive form, and the opening movements include an X-block over the head with a knee raise and then stomping down with a double low block, step punch and chest block, then step and punch (**Figures 57-62**).

Figure 57

Figure 58

Figure 59

Figure 60

Figure 61

Figure 62

This sequence can be used to counter an ambush attack or to regain control of the fight when the enemy is furiously throwing wild punches.

1. You have been surprised by an attack or you have lost control of a fight, and shots are coming in. Thrust both hands up and forward in the X-block position to jam further attacks, protect your head, and to get a sense of where you are in relation to the attacker (**Figure 63**). Through body contact, you should be able to feel where his head, shoulder, and limbs are. You will be either on the left or right side of the attacker—it doesn't matter, as you can adapt the techniques to either side. The kata assumes you are on the attacker's right side, but drill the movements to both sides.
2. Once you get your bearings, wrap one hand around the back of his neck and seize his limb with your other hand, execute a few knee strikes

(**Figure 64**), then stomp down as you hammer down on the back of his neck and pull down on his other arm, ending in the double low-block position (**Figure 65**).
3. Immediately step in if you need to close the distance, pull on his arm (that is the hikite or pull in the kata) and punch to his stomach (**Figure 66**); then strike the side of his head or execute an upper cut punch, ending in the chest-block position (**Figure 67**). Grab a limb and pull (hikite) as you step in and punch (**Figure 68**).
4. Note, the chest-block here can be used to strike or hyper-extend the attacker's elbow joint and then to clear the limb (moving it up and over to the side) as you step in with the punch.
5. Back away defensively and repeat on the other side.

Figure 63

Figure 64

Figure 65

Figure 66

Figure 67

Figure 68

WORKING THE HIKITE

One of the great mysteries of karate training that confound all non-karate martial artists—and even some karateka—is that hand pulled back to the hip or up near the armpit. I distinctly remember a conversation with a young martial artist who had just recently received an instructor's certificate to teach Krav Maga. She confessed that she could not value traditional karate because, in her view, it is so impractical. (I don't think she realized at the time that she was talking to a practical karateka who had been training longer than she had been alive, so I was very interested in how this conversation would play out.) I asked her to please explain why she found karate impractical, and without missing a beat she said that you cannot effectively fight or defend yourself with one hand pulled back "in the pocket" doing nothing.

To her credit, at least she was being analytical. I appreciate anyone willing to analyze a martial art. However, she was attempting analysis with incomplete information, thus arriving at incorrect conclusions. Unfortunately, this misunderstanding is quite common. We must remember that karate has no "dead hands," because karate was designed for in-close, self-defense combat. As such there is never is a hand hanging out doing nothing, and all hand positions and movements in kihon and kata have particular combative functions. The hand pulled back "in the pocket" is called *hikite* in Japanese, usually translated as "pulling hand." Despite what some may claim, this pulling hand is not about generating power. Rather, the hand is pulling and controlling an enemy's limb or some other body part. Or, it is grabbing the enemy for targeting purposes—with a hand on the enemy, you can use proprioception to target your strikes more accurately. When solo training kihon or kata, how do you represent or visualize controlling a limb, pulling down a guard, twisting a shoulder, pulling up a leg, or cranking a head? By pulling the grabbing hand back *as if* you are pulling or controlling the limb. That is *hikite*—pulling hand.

In the bunkai impact training drills outlined and illustrated above, I frequently mention the *hikite* or pulling hand and describe what is being visualized. The classic heavy bag does not have arms and legs (though you can purchase newer heavy bags complete with simulated head, arms, and legs), so you have to *visualize* the limb being manipulated, pulled, and/or moved as you complete the technique. However, if you want to emphasize the *hikite* motion in these drills and really work the pulling hand, then you can improvise the enemy's limb. Note: the Chinese wooden dummy impact training tool has short poles that simulate the enemy's limbs so that practitioners can work in-close fighting techniques such as trapping and pulling limbs as well as attacking joints. Karate was influenced by Chinese fighting systems, particularly Shaolin White Crane Kung Fu, so it makes sense that similar in-close fighting techniques are found in karate. In the absence of a Chinese wooden dummy or a heavy bag with simulated limbs, how might we approximate similar impact training?

We can work the *hikite*—targeting, limb control, and joint attacks—on the heavy bag by using a belt or rope tied around the bag at shoulder level to simulate an arm. You can tie two belts hanging down on opposite sides of the bag to indicate two arms. Or, if you really want to get fancy, you can attach wooden dowels or pipe insulation foam to the bag with bungee cords. In the examples below, I have simply tied a karate belt around my heavy bag. You can start the drills with the belt in your hand, as if you have already grasped the enemy's limb or are already in a clinch scenario. In other drills, you may have to grasp the belt at some point in the sequence as if you are grasping the enemy's arm or wrist. I hope these few examples spark your imagination to create your own *hikite* heavy bag drills!

Basic Punches

1. Hold the belt in one hand as if controlling a limb and pull as you punch the bag multiple times at head and torso levels (**Figure 69**).
2. Reach across and under the belt with the punching hand to transfer the belt (parry and grab motion) (**Figure 70**) and pull as you punch with the other hand (**Figure 71**).
3. Keep transferring the belt back and forth practicing your parry, grab, *hikite*, and punch.
4. At some point, back away defensively.

Figure 69    *Figure 70*    *Figure 71*

High Block Lapel Grab Defense

1. Hold the belt at your own lapel, as if you have grasped the enemy's hand that successfully grabbed your lapel (**Figure 72**).
2. Check in-coming blows with the other hand, then strike the middle of the belt as if you are hitting the crook of the elbow (**Figure 73**).
3. Thrust your forearm into the heavy bag at neck level. You can strike multiple times. (**Figure 74**)
4. Reach back and grasp the middle of the belt as if you are grabbing the crook of the elbow and pull across to your hip as you reverse punch or hook punch at kidney level (**Figure 75**).
5. Grab the bag at face level with the punching hand and knee strike the bag as if you are kneeing the kidneys or lower back (**Figure 76**).
6. Shift your hand to the other side of the bag as if holding the back of the head, let go of the belt, and elbow strike at head level multiple times (**Figure 77**). Back away defensively.

Figure 72

Figure 73

Figure 74

Figure 75

Figure 76

Figure 77

Shuto Strike in Clinch

1. Hold the belt in one hand as if you are grasping the crook of the elbow and grasp the back of the bag with the other hand at neck level, simulating the classic clinch position (**Figure 78**).
2. Strike the back of the bag with your forearm a few times to loosen up the clinch (**Figure 79**) and snake the other arm around the belt as if adjusting the grip to gain control of that arm.
3. Strike the front of the bag at neck/throat level with the forearm as you pull on the belt (**Figure 80**).
4. Imagine the enemy covers his neck to check your strike. With the striking arm, grab the belt and pull down, as if you are pulling down his covering hand, and strike the neck with the other forearm (**Figure 81**).
5. Repeat a few times, switching the belt from one hand to the other.
6. At some point, back away defensively.

Figure 78

Figure 79

Figure 80

Figure 81

Inside Chest Block and Reverse Punch

1. Hold the belt in one hand at head level, as if you just wing blocked a wild punch (**Figure 82**).
2. Reach up with the other hand underneath the belt (**Figure 83**), grab the belt and pull back and down as if to straighten the arm (**Figure 84**), and strike the belt with an inside chest block as if attacking and hyperextending the straightened elbow joint (**Figure 85**). Imagine the enemy is bending over a bit at this point.
3. Grab the belt and pull back as you reverse punch the middle of the bag (**Figure 86**), which is where the enemy's head should be if he were bending over. Back away defensively (**Figure 87**).

Figure 82

Figure 83

Figure 84

Figure 85

Figure 86

Figure 87

Reverse Chest Block, Front Kick, Reverse Punch from Pinan Shodan

1. Hold the belt in one hand and imagine the enemy is reaching in to grab your arm or lapel (**Figure 88**).
2. Step to the outside and feed the belt over to the other hand and grab it, a basic parry-grab move(**Figure 89**), as you step to the side in hook stance and pull the belt back into chest block position (**Figure 90**). You are using the chest block motion to pull the enemy forward and off balance, or at least shifting his weight forward.
3. Kick at knee level as if kicking out one of his legs as you pull belt (**Figure 91**).
4. Pull the belt and reverse punch multiple times (**Figure 92**).
5. Back away defensively (**Figure 93**).

Figure 88

Figure 89

Figure 90

Figure 91

Figure 92

Figure 93

Conclusion

These are just a few examples of bunkai impact training drills. Explore your kata, forms, and other self-defense drills from your system, and figure out fun and creative ways to work those techniques on a heavy bag or a Bob training dummy. Not only will you develop speed, power, and body dynamics in your bunkai or self-defense techniques, but the process of exploring your kata and forms and creating your own bunkai impact training drills will deepen your understanding of your system's combative principles.

Author performing kata Wankan in a heavy bag-kata combination drill

6 COMBINING TRAINING METHODS

FLEXIBILITY OF SOLO TRAINING

Training like a modern day ronin means you can train the way you want. No one else is criticizing your routines or saying you are wrong for training a certain way. Of course, that does not mean you can just do anything imaginable, because of various limitations: your body condition, your age, training locations, time restrictions, and available training equipment. But, beyond these reasonable constraints, your training is as wide open as your imagination.

Unlike group or partner training that may be scheduled at particular times, conducted in specific places, determined by the sensei or instructor, and contingent upon other people or partners, solo training is completely flexible. You can train on your own schedule, practice for as long or short as you want, and determine your own training contexts and content. For me, the true joy of solo training is being able to concentrate on what interests me the most, and digging deeper into aspects of my training that I find most important at that point in my martial arts development.

COMBINATIONALISM IN TRAINING

In the previous chapters, we explored specific types of solo training, including warming up and cooling down, kihon practice with a view toward practical application of techniques, kata or forms training in conjunction with practical bunkai practice, and impact training. In this chapter, we will review some creative ways of combining these different training methods to diversify your solo training. Indeed, sometimes you will want to focus on specific elements of training for extended periods of time. You may want to spend a week or a month just working your kata and bunkai. At other times, you may decide to drill your kihon or develop your impact training for several sessions or weeks in a row. Sometimes your training will indeed be very specific and focused on specific modalities.

However, you may also decide to vary your sessions to stave off boredom or to keep from becoming stuck in a training rut. One danger is becoming bored and unmotivated, and that can lead to lapses in your training. Learning to combine training routines in creative yet meaningful ways can keep your solo practice fresh and engaging, while also encouraging you to achieve your training goals. Review your different types of training, and then mix and match them in new and interesting ways. Be sure to keep your overarching training goals in mind, and then combine your routines. Below are a few examples of training sessions I've created. Hopefully, they will serve as inspiration for you to create your own training combinations.

Kihon and Kata Training

1. Start with a brief warmup that increases the heart rate, warms the major muscles and joints, and that includes some ballistic stretching of key muscle groups.
2. Choose a kata or form and identify key techniques or movements that distinguish that kata.
3. Practice those key techniques with kihon exercises, performing at least ten repetitions using the appropriate stance as in the kata, moving up and down the floor or by switching your feet and remaining in place if you have limited space.
4. Perform the kata at slow motion, focusing on technique and body positioning.
5. Perform the kata at full speed and power, focusing on body dynamics.
6. Choose another kata, and drill key techniques as kihon exercises, followed by performing the kata slowly and then at full speed and power.
7. Continue with various kata, for as much time as you have for that training session.
8. Finish with a cool down, including static stretching.

Kihon, Kata, and Application Training

1. Begin with a warmup that includes light shadow boxing hand, elbow, knee, and kicking techniques.
2. Identify several basic techniques at the core of your system (e.g., punches, high blocks, inside and outside chest blocks, low blocks, knife-hand blocks, front kicks, side kicks, roundhouse kicks, inside and outside crescent kicks, and hook kicks).
3. Drill each one separately, first in traditional kihon style and then shadow boxing a practical application of that technique.
4. Once you have worked through all the kihon techniques, start on your kata.
5. Perform the kata with full speed and power. Then, shadow box a few practical bunkai from that kata.
6. Work through as many kata as you can, given your training session time limit.
7. Finish with a cool down that includes static stretching.

Heavy Bag and Kata Circuit Training

1. Begin with a brief but comprehensive warmup.
2. Work several reps of a heavy-bag combination.
3. Perform a kata first slowly and then at full speed and power.
4. Work several reps of another heavy-bag combination.
5. Perform a different kata, first slowly and then at full speed and power.
6. Continue alternating heavy-bag combinations and kata practice until your training time has ended.
7. Finish with a cool down that includes static stretching.

Kata, Bunkai Shadow Boxing, and Heavy Bag Circuits

1. Begin with a brief but comprehensive warmup that includes ballistic stretching.
2. Using an interval timer, create a series of one-minute circuits with 15 seconds of rest between each circuit.
3. First circuit: perform a kata or form at full speed and power; keep repeating the kata until the minute circuit ends.

4. Second circuit: pick a few practical bunkai applications from that kata or form and shadow box them, alternating your lead leg, until the minute circuit ends.
5. Third circuit: work a heavy-bag combination, alternating your lead leg, until the minute circuit ends. Consider including practical bunkai combinations based upon the kata or form you performed.
6. Continue this basic circuit training pattern, working through various kata or forms, until the training time ends.
7. Finish with a cool down that includes static stretching.

Kata and Bunkai Heavy Bag Workout

1. Begin with a brief but comprehensive warmup that includes ballistic stretching.
2. Perform a kata in slow motion, visualizing your bunkai applications.
3. Perform the kata at full speed and power.
4. Pick one bunkai sequence and practice it ten times on the heavy bag, alternating your lead leg.
5. You can focus on one kata and work as many bunkai applications as you can (the ones that work well on a heavy bag or Bob dummy); or, you can choose one bunkai sequence from each of your kata, working through the kata and applications until your training time is up.
6. Finish with a cool down that includes static stretching.

Thirty-Minute Martial Arts Workout

This workout is an intense training session that combines a variety of martial arts exercises and techniques. I adopted the one below from a similar workout created by Iain Abernethy as described in one of his podcasts. Use this as a basic template to create your own routine, focusing on the techniques that relate to your own martial arts training.

Start with a basic warm up that includes ballistic stretching.

1. One minute of light shadow boxing with punching only, using different punches and palm-heel strikes (jabs, crosses, hooks, upper cuts, palm-heels, and slaps).
2. One minute of punches, elbow strikes (upward, cross, and downward),

and knee strikes—create practical combinations.
3. One minute of adding in kicks—punches, elbows, knees, various kicks (include practical kicks at knee, thigh, and groin level).
4. One minute of crunches or any other abdominal exercise.
5. One minute of rest (move around, throw a few light, slow punches, and breathe).
6. One minute of ten reps of the following in side stance (do as many of these you can within one minute):
   - 10 punches
   - 10 palm-heel strikes
   - 10 round house elbow strikes
   - 10 chest blocks
   - 10 low blocks
7. One minute of pushups.
8. One minute of rest (move around, throw a few light, slow punches, and breathe).
9. One minute of hand combinations (jab, double jabs, jab-cross, jab-cross-hook, straight punches, etc.) .
10. One minute of back lifts (on stomach, lift your upper body and your feet off the ground).
11. One minute of rest (move around, throw a few light, slow punches, and breathe).
12. One minute of light shadow boxing, moving around, but keep it light and maintain good form.
13. One minute of rest (move around, throw a few light, slow punches, and breathe).
14. One minute of jab-cross-hook-cross as hard and fast as you can without stopping, flowing each technique together. You can switch the lead foot after each repetition.
15. One minute of slow kata practice, paying attention to technique; if you finish the kata, start again until end of one minute or do some light shadow fighting.
16. One minute of regular speed kata practice.
17. One minute of slow kata practice.
18. One minute of squats or lunges.
19. One minute of jumping back and forth over a mark or towel or spot on the floor; keep the feet together and hop back and forth.
20. One minute of rest (move around, throw a few light, slow punches, and breathe).

21. One minute of left leg lifts as if winding up for a front kick or round kick or side kick—you can vary these leg lift windups.
22. One minute of right leg lifts as if winding up for front kick or round kick or side kick— you can vary these leg lift windups.
23. One minute of alternating leg lifts.
24. One minute of light shadow fighting (hand, elbow, knee, and feet techniques), very gentle.
25. One minute of light shadow boxing, hands only.

Note: If you have a heavy bag, strike and kick the heavy bag instead of striking and kicking the air.

Finish with some gentle static stretching.

Fifteen-Minute Martial Arts Workout

If you are pressed for time, consider this short, intense martial arts workout. I adopted this workout from a similar one created by Iain Abernethy as described in one of his podcasts. Use this as a basic template to create your own routine, focusing on the techniques that relate to your own martial arts training. Using an interval timer, create several thirty-second circuits with ten-second rests between each main circuit.

Start with a basic warm up that includes ballistic stretching.

1. Jumping jacks
2. Squat kicks (front kicks)
3. Pushups
4. Crunches
5. Jab, cross, hook, cross and switch feet
6. Lunges (hands in guard)
7. Plank
8. Push up with rotation (lift one arm up to ceiling and look at hand)
9. Continuous left lead round house kick
10. Spotty Dog (Jumping with feet moving front and back as the hands alternate, moving up and down)
11. Slow push ups
12. Wall squats
13. Lead elbow, back elbow, knee and switch feet

14. Sit throughs (push up position, lift right arm and swing left leg to the side and touch left hip to floor, back to push up position and do other side)
15. Continuous right lead round house kick
16. Left side plank
17. High knees (running in place lifting knees)
18. Punches in side stance
19. Right side plank
20. Pushups with lifting hand to side (like hikite)
21. Front kick forward, side kick to the side, keeping knee up (alternate legs)
22. Jumping squats
23. Standing deep breaths slowly raising arms up and down as in jumping jacks

Note: If you have a heavy bag, strike and kick the heavy bag instead of striking and kicking the air.

Finish with some gentle static stretching.

Fifteen-Minute Martial Arts Workout Followed by Kata Practice

If you have a nice block of time, at least thirty minutes, consider combining the fifteen-minute martial arts workout described above with fifteen minutes (or more) of kata practice. When I want a killer thirty-minute workout, I will start with the fifteen-minute martial arts workout and then do about fifteen minutes of intense kata practice, working as many kata at full speed and power as I can within the remaining time. Try it! I guarantee you will be exhausted by the end.

Conclusion

Combining different routines not only helps you vary your training regimen, but it also allows you to control the level of exertion and exhaustion within your workouts. If performed at constant high intensity, these routines are excellent training for fighting through exhaustion and coping with adrenaline reactions. As you become more exhausted, and as more adrenaline is pumped into your system, it becomes harder to control your fine motor movements. Trying to perform the intricate and complicated movements of kata or forms, for example, while exhausted is excellent training for that self-defense confrontation in which you must fight hard through exhaustion and to strike as effectively as possible under duress in order to get to safety.

God forbid any of us should have to use our training. But, sometimes awareness, avoidance, escape, and de-escalation do not work, and we may find ourselves in a violent confrontation. We need to be physically fit and prepared for such civilian combat. These kinds of intensive solo training routines, along with training hard with non-compliant partners (in controlled, safe scenarios monitored by an experienced instructor or sensei), can help prepare us for such self-defense situations.

Author doing bicep curls on gravity straps

7 CARDIO AND STRENGTH TRAINING

Fit to Fight

Whatever your preferred martial arts training context happens to be, you should be in good enough shape to fight, escape, and flee. In self-defense, the ultimate goal is not to have to fight at all. Practicing such self-protection skills as awareness, avoidance, de-escalation, and escape is essential training for self-defense contexts.

Physical violence is always unpredictable. If you engage in a physical confrontation, chances are you will be injured in some way, from minor scrapes and bruises to major, life-altering bodily injury, as well as experiencing emotional, psychological, and spiritual damage. As Sun Tzu reminds us in *The Art of War*, the best battles are those won without ever having to fight.

However, there are times when awareness, avoidance, and de-escalation fail such that escape is impossible. During such times, fighting is necessary, and you must be prepared to fight with all your might to end the altercation quickly and to escape as safely as possible with as little injury as possible. You must be in good physical condition to be able to fight off your attacker(s) and to run for safety. Physical conditioning is key.

If self-defense is not your main training context, you still need to maintain good physical conditioning. Those who are training for competition, especially kumite, but also kata, weapons, and group demonstrations, must also be in top physical shape to compete successfully. You know your competitors are hitting the gym to build strength and stamina to win in the ring. Neglecting your own physical training will only give unnecessary advantages to your opponents.

Incorporate various physical conditioning exercises to help you succeed in your competition goals.

Even those who mainly train for the martial arts context, for pure enjoyment of body movement, personal improvement, and good health should also consider some kind of physical conditioning routine. Indeed, your dojo workouts may be intense enough to provide good cardio and some strength training. However, if you include physical conditioning outside the dojo, you will notice that your martial arts will greatly improve. Your techniques will be stronger, your form will be sharper, your recovery after workouts will be quicker, and your ability to learn new movements and techniques will be improved. Whatever your martial arts context—self-defense, sport, or personal development—your training will be enhanced if you add quality physical conditioning.

Ronin training lends itself to physical conditioning. Indeed, some people need to exercise with partners to maintain proper motivation and achieve specific training goals. Some need a training coach to teach them exercises, check their form, and motivate them to succeed. But, if you are already training by yourself in your martial arts, then you probably already have the discipline to persevere in personal physical conditioning.

Also, you do not necessarily need expensive equipment. Sure, you can join a gym with fancy exercise apparatus, or you can spend loads of money on your own home gym, or you can simply run outside and use your own body weight as resistance, for just the cost of running shoes and training attire. However and wherever you decide to exercise, your physical conditioning should include cardio exercises and strength training, and ideally, you should combine elements of both.

Note: Before starting any cardio or weight training exercise, consult your physician.

CARDIO EXERCISES

Cardio exercise provides many excellent health and training benefits. It increases stamina to allow you to train harder and longer in your martial art and increases your ability to escape danger and run to safety during a self-defense situation. Cardio exercising strengthens your heart and lungs, and depending upon the type of cardio exercise you do, it can work the major muscle groups of the body. Cardio work is great for burning calories, reducing body fat, and reaching weight-loss goals. The three types of cardio exercise we will discuss include swimming, running, and cycling.

Swimming

Swimming generally gives you the most intense cardio sessions, because it works your entire body. Swimming, to my mind, is the best cardio workout, ever. But, there are a few drawbacks. Obviously, you need to know how to swim. Secondly, you need a clean body of water in which to swim. If you live near the ocean, a lake, or a clean pond, then swimming out in nature can be wonderful. But your workouts will depend upon the weather. Unless you are in the polar bear club, it's no fun swimming outside on a bitterly cold winter day. Also, it's just not a good idea to swim during a rain storm, especially if lightening is involved. Pools are your best bet. But, you need access to a pool, preferably an indoor one. Your local gym, YMCA, college, or high school may offer community access to a pool for swimming laps. In all cases, avoid swimming alone or without supervision.

Start slowly, and gradually build up your endurance. Be sure to do some ballistic stretching and warmups before you swim. Learn the pool etiquette, and avoid being that annoying person crossing lanes or zigzagging along making it difficult for everyone else trying to get in their laps.

Running

If you are not a swimmer, or do not have access to a pool, or simply do not like swimming, then running is a great option. Running mainly works your legs, hips, and core, and it provides an excellent cardio workout. However, running is much more strenuous on your joints than swimming. Your feet, ankles, knees, and hips take a real pounding, and your lower back can be stressed as well. If you decide to run, consider paying a little extra for quality running shoes that absorb some of the shock of running.

Ideally, you should run outside, especially if you live out in the country, or in a pleasant suburb or neighborhood. It's wonderful to get out and breathe fresh air and enjoy the natural surroundings. Also, these outdoor settings sometimes provide hills, turns, and a variety of scenery to make the running experience more enjoyable. Not everyone lives in the country, and I know plenty of people who run in big cities. But, you need to be careful of cars, bicycles, and other pedestrians, and sometimes air quality can be poor.

Also, running outdoors makes you dependent upon the weather. Avoid running in extreme heat or cold. Avoid running at night or in rain storms, as it is more difficult for drivers to see you, and for you to see them. If you must run at night, practice good safety, awareness, and self-protection: wear reflective clothing, stay alert, avoid secluded paths and trails, and do not wear earbuds and listen to loud music, which distracts you from situational awareness. If running outdoors is not a feasible option, look for an indoor running track at a local gym, the YMCA, or a local high school or college. Another option is to use a treadmill or an elliptical, either at home or at a gym or the YMCA. Such running can be really boring, but at least it is safe, and you can listen to an audio book, or get caught up on your Netflix binge-watching, or listen to your favorite martial arts podcast.

As with swimming, ease into running. Be sure to start with some light warmups and ballistic stretching. If you haven't ever run before or have not run in many years, listen to your body and ignore your ego. Start with half a mile or one mile. Consider alternating between running and walking until your stamina increases such that you can run the whole distance. Instead of focusing on distance at first, you can run for a set period of time. Start with 20 minutes and gradually increase the time.

Note: If you run outdoors, consider varying your routine days, times, and routes, for self-protection purposes. And, maintain situational awareness at all times, especially if running alone.

Cycling

Of these three primary cardio activities, cycling can be the most dynamic and fun. (Who doesn't like flying down hills on a country road as trees and fields zip by?) However, you need to know how to ride a bike, and cycling can be expensive and troublesome. You need a good multispeed bicycle, and really good ones can run hundreds, even thousands of dollars. You should also wear safety equipment, like a helmet and possibly elbow and knee pads. (Falling off a speeding bike can be very painful and injurious, even deadly!)

You also need a nice place to ride. If you want a touring cycle cardio experience, then you'll need several kilometers of smooth, well-paved roadway. If you want the more rugged off-road mountain-bike experience, then you'll need to find a park with biking trails. In most cases, you'll need to travel to these biking trails, in which case you'll need to have a bicycle rack for your vehicle. Yeah, cycling can provide an amazing cardio workout, but for many people, it's just too costly and bothersome.

Like running outdoors, cycling depends upon weather. Rainstorms, heavy winds, extreme heat or cold, and snow provide environmental challenges to the avid cyclist. As with running, there are indoor cycling options. You can go to a gym and ride a stationary bike, and some are quite sophisticated, with display monitors that provide various information like speed, heart rate, and calories burned. Some even have programmed routes that simulate road conditions, incline, and decline. If you care to spend some money, you can purchase one for your home gym. Or, you can purchase a relatively inexpensive indoor cycling trainer stand, which allows you to transform your bike into a stationary bike. Most training stands come equipped with resistance settings so you can increase the cardio intensity of your cycling sessions.

Cycling can be very intense on your body and cardiovascular system, so make sure you ease into a cycling workout regimen. Start with a basic warmup, making sure your lower back, hips, knees, and ankles are suitably warmed up. Consider some ballistic stretching, especially for the hips and hamstrings. As with any exercise routine, start out modestly and gradually increase the intensity and distance. Instead of focusing on distance, consider cycling for set time periods. Start off with 20 minutes and work up from there. Also, you can have a set time period, say 30 minutes, and gradually increase the distance you ride during that set time period.

Note: If you cycle outdoors, consider varying your routine days, times, and routes, for self-protection purposes. And, maintain situational awareness at all times, especially if cycling alone.

Cardio workouts should be a regular part of your individual training. However, be wise. Don't overdo it, and listen to your body. If you are exhausted, then slow down and gradually cease the workout. Avoid abruptly ending a cardio workout, unless absolutely necessary (as when injury is involved). If you start feeling sharp pain in your muscles or joints, then make adjustments in your movement to alleviate the pain, change your activity, or cease the activity for that day and rest. If pain persists, consult your primary care physician.

Throughout any cardio routine, hydrate yourself. Avoid drinking large quantities of water or sports drinks beforehand. Rather, drink small amounts before and during the workout. At the end, you can drink larger portions. Plan a cooldown to end the cardio session. Walking for a few minutes followed by light stretching works well. Or, do a few kata (forms) at medium or slow pace and/or some light shadow boxing, followed by some light stretching. The idea is to bring your heartrate and body temperature down gradually after the intense cardio workout.

As with any activity, especially if you are running, cycling, or swimming outdoors, consider varying your routine days, times, and routes for self-protection purposes. Doing the same thing at set times on the same days makes you a predictable target for criminals and attackers.

STRENGTH TRAINING

In addition to cardio workouts, your ronin training should also include some form of strength training. Whereas cardio training increases stamina, conditions muscles for extended exertion, and strengthens the heart and lungs, strength training builds muscle, enabling you to generate more power in your techniques. Strength training also makes the body more resilient and able to absorb impact force. If you are ever attacked in a self-defense situation, you will need as much physical strength as possible to deliver devastating blows and to take impact from your attacker (most likely, you will take hits if you are in a self-defense altercation).

Effective strength training involves weight-resistance exercise. In this section, we will briefly examine four types: traditional Okinawan weight training, contemporary weight training, gravity straps, and body-weight resistance training.

Traditional Okinawan Exercises

Classical Okinawan weight training includes exercising with such pieces of equipment as *chishi*, *sashi*, *kami*, and *tetsugeta*. The *chishi* is an ancient type of dumbbell that looks like a stone attached to the end of a wooden handle. You can make these with wooden dowels and concrete poured into a plastic bucket to varying depths depending upon how heavy you want the weight. Just trim the plastic bucket away once the concrete has hardened. These weights are used to increase grip, forearm, shoulder, chest, and upper back strength to improve power in gripping and striking.

Sashi look like our contemporary cowbell weights, and are usually made of iron, stone, or concrete. These weights can be held when punching to increase arm, shoulder, chest, and upper back strength to increase power in striking and gripping.

Kami are ceramic jars used to store grain, rice, or wine. You can fill these jars with varying amounts of sand, pebbles, water, or rice depending upon the desired weight. *Kami* are generally used to increase grip, forearm, and shoulder strength to improve power in gripping, tearing, and striking.

Tetsugeta are weighted clogs or sandals made from iron, stone, or concreted, and they are used to increase leg strength and to produce more powerful stances and kicks.

Browse YouTube and other online resources to find effective exercises utilizing these traditional Okinawan weight-training tools.

Contemporary Weight Training

The basic principle of weight training is to use weighted objects against gravity to provide resistance to make the muscles work harder. From this basic principle, dozens of schools of thought have developed regarding best practices in weight training. Note that there are differences between "body building" and strength training. The former seeks to bulk, shape, tone, and "cut" the body to give a certain look. The latter seeks to build power and strength. When weight training, be sure to follow an exercise regimen designed to increase strength and power in your martial arts techniques without impeding flexibility and range of motion through bulk or being "muscle bound" (that is, to be limited in movement due to size of muscle mass).

Most trainers and weight-training specialists agree that free weights are the most effective for building strength and power. However, free weights can be dangerous, so never use them alone. Always have a partner to serve as a spotter. Ronin training often occurs in isolation, making free weight training difficult. But, you can join a gym or your local YMCA and make use of free weights in a safe environment. Browse the Internet and YouTube to find effective free-weight training routines designed for martial artists.

As an alternative to free weights, you can use various forms of universal weight machines. These pieces of equipment still use weights and gravity to produce resistance, but they are generally safer to use, especially for novice weight trainers. Changing the weight resistance is much simpler on machine devices, often involving nothing more than moving a metal pin. However, because the machines are designed to be used in specific ways, the types of exercises can be limited, and you may not get the same range of motion out of the exercises as with free weights. But weight machines are efficient and very effective for most martial arts training purposes. Though machines are generally safer than free weights, it is still a good idea to have a spotter or to work out in a gym setting where others can assist you if needed. Browse the Internet and YouTube for fun and effective weight machine workouts designed for martial artists.

Gravity Straps

For the ronin who cannot go to the gym or the local YMCA to use free weights or exercise machines, gravity straps are an excellent alternative. Gravity straps are relatively inexpensive, compact, easily stored, and can be used while traveling. All you need are the straps and a strong door. (You can also attach them to cross beams in your basement, garage, or shed.) These straps are multifunctional and use your own body weight as the source of resistance.

You can work all major muscle groups in a short period of time and in a compact space. Exercises include squats, rows, chest presses (bench press), bicep curls, triceps extensions, butterfly extensions, stomach crunches, and a variety of other exercises and variations. Most brands come with a basic exercise manual, and you can find more exercise routines online or on YouTube. Gravity straps are also excellent for circuit training regimens.

Basic Body-Weight Resistance Training

If for whatever reason you do not want to bother with using any equipment whatsoever, then you can perform basic body-weight resistance exercises. The classic pushup, pullup (may require minimal equipment), sit up, and crunch exercises are excellent for quality resistance training. Since you are only working with your own body weight, you need to be creative in changing up the reps and body positioning to get the most out of your workouts.

For example, the Navy Seal workout uses the pyramid rep system, in which you perform one rep, then two, then three, all the way up to ten and then back down to one. You'll never look at pushups the same again after one set of pyramid style pushups. Changing the elevation of your feet, or shifting the position of your hands in relation to your feet (for example, the Spider Man pushup) will also give you a variety of exercises. The Internet and YouTube have hundreds of amazing exercises and routines you can use.

As with any exercise routine, make sure you are well hydrated before and during your weight-training activities. Also, take some time to warmup before exercising. You can do a short run, for example, to get the blood pumping and to prime your body for the workout. Also, ballistic stretching of the limbs and joints you plan to exercise is important to prevent injury. After your workout, be sure to have a cool down routine. I like to do a few slow-motion or medium-paced kata, light shadow boxing, and some light stretching.

Combining Routines

I'm a big fan of combining training routines, and I do the same for cardio and strength training. Sometimes I devote certain days to cardio training and others for weight training. For example, I may do different types of cardio workouts (running, kata, heavy bag routines, bunkai training) on Mondays, Wednesdays, and Fridays and my gravity strap workouts on Tuesdays and Thursdays. Other times, I may combine the workouts, doing cardio for half the session and then weight training for the other half (or vice versa). Note: If you run or cycle outdoors, consider varying the days, times, and routes of your routines as much as possible, for self-protection purposes.

Or, I may include short cardio exercises as part of my gravity strap circuit training or weight machine circuits. For example, most of my circuit training includes 45 seconds of resistance exercise followed by 25 seconds rest. When combining cardio with the circuit training, I'll include some "active rest" periods. Between the major exercises during the rest periods, I might do such things as the following:

- running in place
- jumping jacks or squat jumps
- shadow boxing
- practical bunkai and kihon combinations in the air or on the heavy bag
- kicking combinations in the air or on a heavy bag
- perform as much of a kata as I can at full speed and power

CONCLUSION

Remember that resistance training and cardio workouts achieve different outcomes. Resistance training builds strength. Cardio workouts burn more calories and develops stamina. To get the most out of your training, reflect on your workout purposes and the context of your martial arts training, and then develop the best possible cardio and weight training routines to help you achieve your goals.

Author with Shorin Ryu Karate Do International (SRKDI) Yudansha at Honbu Dojo in Okinawa, 2015

CONCLUSION

Context, Context, Context

We started our exploration of solo training by discussing some of the reasons we might find ourselves in the position of modern ronin. Some folks may have moved to a new location and are still searching for a dojo or martial arts school in which to continue training. Others, unfortunately, may have had a falling out with a school, sensei, or organization, and find themselves without a martial arts home, training solo while seeking out new affiliations. Still, others may just be seeking ways to supplement their group martial arts training, focusing on specific techniques and exploring personal training goals.

Also, many advanced students and instructors who run their own dojos or martial arts schools set time aside to continue their own training. Ideally, such individuals should train with a more advanced instructor, but sometimes that is not always possible, due to location and training schedule conflicts. Solo training is necessary for the instructor to continue growing as a martial artist.

Whatever the reason you find yourself to be a modern day ronin, always keep in mind the importance of training for context. Our training never occurs in a vacuum; we never train devoid of some kind of martial context. Whatever the context may be, we should develop our solo training routines accordingly. By way of conclusion, I would like to discuss some common training contexts and provide suggestions and tips on how to apply the strategies in this book to these different training situations.

Martial Arts Context

Most martial artists—those who devote a significant amount of their lives to studying the martial arts—train primarily for the martial arts context. That is, they enjoy exploring the full range of elements that make up the martial arts, including physical training, intellectual study of combative principles, cultural and historical analysis of the systems in which they train, and the aesthetics of body movement. The true martial artist recognizes there is much more to training than just learning how to fight—the body, mind, and spirit are all explored, developed, and, hopefully, improved over a lifetime of study and training.

For well-rounded martial artists, all of the solo training drills and activities outlined in this book will be applicable at varying times and to varying degrees throughout their martial training:

- Kihon training will further develop power, speed, body dynamics, and aesthetics in each technique.
- Kata practice will enhance speed and power, understanding of the application of the techniques, understanding of the relationships between various techniques in transition, and a deeper awareness of body dynamics as they relate to beauty in form and function of the sequences.
- Impact training will strengthen the techniques (increase power), improve eye-hand coordination, and sharpen the relationship between form and function of each technique.
- Concentrating on the application of kihon and bunkai in kata will stimulate the martial imagination and deepen the academic and practical understanding of how the movements can be applied to civilian combat.
- Strength and cardio training provides essential physical and mental support for all aspects of martial arts study and practice.

Personal Development Context

Some people pursue the martial arts as a way to improve the self. There is always a new technique to learn, a new kata or form to master, another belt rank to earn, or another martial principle to explore. In the personal development context, the true fight is within. According to Shoshin Nagamine, "Karate-do may be referred to as the conflict within yourself, or a life-long marathon which can be won only through self-discipline, hard training, and your own creative efforts."[1] And, the widely quoted statement attributed to Gichin Funakoshi illustrates this personal development context well: "The ultimate aim of karate lies not in victory or defeat, but in the perfection of the character of its participants."

Most modern martial arts schools, especially those billing themselves as traditional martial arts, facilitate the goal of personal development by following some kind of belt rank system (note, ranking systems were not part of the ancient, traditional martial arts but is a modern development ironically associated with traditional martial arts). Such ranking systems allow individuals to set goals and measure their personal progress. In this way, the student continually battles with the person in the mirror.

Solo training can facilitate preparing for promotion exams or simply improving oneself according to established personal goals:

- Kihon training helps sharpen and improve your individual techniques.
- Kata practice develops your kata performance and helps you prepare for the next rank test.
- Impact training will develop your speed, power, agility, and strength.
- Solo training your kihon applications and kata bunkai will improve your ability to apply the techniques in a self-defense situation, bolstering your personal confidence in the efficacy of your training.
- Strength and cardio training improves physical, mental, and emotional health and prepares you for the challenges of weekly martial arts training and periodic promotion tests.

Competitive Sports Context

The martial arts were not developed for the purposes of competitive sport as understood and experienced today. Rather, all martial arts were, well, martial in their origin. In English, we gain our word *martial* from the Roman mythic figure Mars, the god of war. The various martial arts were all developed for either civilian combat (self-defense) or for military combat in service of the ruler and the protection of the tribe, clan, country, kingdom, or empire.

However, we should acknowledge that even within these martial, military contexts, there were still games of sorts. Think, for example, of knightly

---

[1] Nagamine, *The Essence of Okinawan Karate-Do*, p. 47.

tournaments in Europe, or the traditional boxing matches between Thai warriors. Indeed, sport elements in these ancient martial arts existed, but the primary purpose was always combative, either civilian or military.

In modern times, the martial arts can be studied and pursued primarily for competitive reasons. Tournaments involving kata, kumite (sparring), weapons, and self-defense demonstrations are extremely popular and well attended. Judo, Taekwondo, and wrestling are in the Olympics, and Karate debuted in the Tokyo Summer Olympics (originally set for 2020 but postponed until 2021 due to the COVID-19 global pandemic).

Solo training for sport martial arts is a vital aspect of preparing for any competition:

- Kata and kihon practice will sharpen your form, speed, power, and aesthetic timing to help you perform your best tournament kata or form.
- Impact training develops speed, power, timing and strength for your sparring matches or cage fights.
- Strength and cardio training develops speed, power, and endurance for competition.

Practical Self-Defense Context

A significant number of people, mainly adults, start studying the martial arts because they want to learn how to protect themselves and their loved ones from violent assault. In response, some modern, practical self-defense martial arts have emerged within the last two or three decades, billing themselves as the ultimate system for street self-defense. Most martial arts schools make some claim to teaching self-defense. And, karate dojos that teach practical application of the kata movements prepare their students for protecting themselves in an actual violent confrontation in the street.

Of course, any martial art school that teaches "self-defense" should also explain to students that the physical techniques of self-defense is only about five to ten percent of self-protection, and they should also be teaching information about awareness, avoidance, de-escalation, escape, and legal, medical, psychological, and emotional consequences of violence.

The solo training strategies outlined in this book, if pursued appropriately, can greatly enhance your self-defense training:

- Kihon practice that emphasizes practical application will allow you to analyze your basics for self-defense application and to practice them safely.
- Kata practice that focuses on practical bunkai teaches you how to pull the self-defense techniques from the forms and gives you opportunity to practice the techniques at full speed and power, developing body dynamics, working the inside and outside of your attacker, moving at various angles in relation to your attacker, and developing effective and practical combinations that will help you fight off an attacker and escape safely.
- Bunkai impact training gives you opportunity to practice your self-defense techniques at full speed and power without risk of harming a partner. (Of course, you must also train bunkai and self-defense techniques with partners in compliant and non-compliant drills in the presence of an experienced instructor.) Moreover, impact training helps you develop speed, power, and accuracy in executing your techniques.
- Strength and cardio training develops physical and emotional fitness, preparing you to persevere through self-defense situations in which you must fight to escape and/or to protect others from harm and to facilitate their safe escape.

Combination of Contexts

Finally, a great many martial artists actually train for a variety of reasons, shifting between contexts at different phases of their training and their life-long journey through the martial arts. Some may begin the martial arts as a child and train primarily for competition through their teens and into their early twenties, then shift more towards the self-defense contexts as they mature and start families, and then move into a martial arts context as they grow older. Others may maintain martial arts, sport, and self-defense contexts throughout much of their lifetime of training. Still others may begin for the purpose of self-development and then use other contexts, like sport, self-defense, and martial arts, to further enhance their primary self-development context.

Solo training can greatly benefit those who train with many contexts in mind. Whatever context you happen to be training at any given time in your martial arts life, be creative and consider how you might mix and match the different solo training exercises and drills described in this book to help you reach and even exceed your specific training goals.

Conclusion

The beauty of the martial arts is that there is no one way to pursue training. The martial arts are as varied as the people who practice and study them. As such, there is no one "right" or "best" way to train like a ronin. Reflect upon your own martial arts training goals, review the principles and training ideas discussed in this book, and develop solo training routines that best suit your interests, fit your various training contexts, and help you achieve your martial arts goals.

I trust this book has revealed a few (hopefully, many!) ideas that you can use, and I hope that some discussions and examples have sparked your martial imagination to create your own exercises and routines. My sincerest wish is that this book can play an important part in your own personal development as a martial artist and that it will encourage you to get out there and train like a ronin.

BIBLIOGRAPHY

Abernethy, Iain. *Bunkai Jutsu: The Practical Application of Karate Kata*. Cockermouth, UK: NETH Publishing, 2002. Kindle AZW file.

Clarke, Christopher. *American Shorin-Ryu Karate Association: A Manual for Students and Instructors*. 3rd Ed. Fort Washington, MD: ASKA Press, 1989.

Consterdine, Peter. *Streetwise: The Complete Manual of Personal Security and Self Defence*. Leeds, UK: Protection Publications, 1997.

De Becker, Gavin. *The Gift of Fear: Survival Signals That Protect Us from Violence*. New York: Dell, 1997.

Fraguas, Jose M. *Karate Masters*, vol. 5. Los Angeles: Empire Books, 2014.

Funakoshi, Gichin. *Karate-Do Kyohan: The Master Text*. New York: Kodansha, 1973.

———. *Karate-Do Nyumon: The Master Introductory Text*. New York: Kodansha, 1988.

Itosu, Anko. "The 10 Precepts of Anko Itosu." *Iain Abernethy: The Practical Application of Karate*. Accessed February 10, 2016. http://www.iainabernethy.co.uk/article/10-precepts-anko-itosu.

Kane, Lawrence and Kris Wilder. *The Little Black Book of Violence: What Every Young Man Needs to Know about Fighting*. Wolfeboro, NH: YMAA Publication Center, 2009.

Kennedy, Brian and Elizabeth Guo. *Chinese Martial Arts Training Manuals: A Historical Survey*. Berkeley, CA: Blue Snake Books, 2005.

McCarthy, Patrick. *Bubishi: The Classic Manual of Combat*. Tokyo: Tuttle, 2008.

McMillan, Danny, et. al. "Dynamic vs. Static-Stretching Warm Up: The Effect on Power and Agility Performance. *Journal of Strength and Conditioning Research* 20, no. 3 (2006). http://journals.lww.com.

Miller, Rory. *Facing Violence: Preparing for the Unexpected*. Wolfeboro, NH: YMAA Publication Center, 2011.

———. *Meditations on Violence: A Comparison of Martial Arts Training and Real World Violence*. Wolfeboro, NH: YMAA Publication Center, 2008.

Miller, Rory and Lawrence Kane. *Scaling Force: Dynamic Decision-Making Under Threat of Violence*. Wolfeboro, NH: YMAA Publication Center, 2012.

Motobu, Choki. *Okinawan Karate*. Ontario: Masters Publication, 1995.

Nagamine, Shoshin. *The Essence of Okinawan Karate-Do*. Rutland, VT: Tuttle, 1976.

———. *Tales of Okinawa's Great Masters*. Boston: Tuttle, 2000.

Thompson, Geoff. *Dead or Alive; It's Your Choice: The Definitive Self-Protection Handbook*. Boulder, CO: Paladin Press, 1997.

ABOUT THE AUTHOR

David S. Hogsette earned his Ph.D. in English Language and Literature at The Ohio State University, where he first started training in Matsubayashi Shorin-ryu. He is Professor of English and the adviser for the martial arts club at the college where he teaches literature and writing. On occasion, he teaches a practical karate physical education course and leads self-protection and self-defense seminars at the college and in the local community. He holds the rank of 4th Dan in Matsubayashi Shorin-ryu and 1st Dan in Shotokan Karate, and he is the founder and head instructor for the Shorin Ryu Karate Academy (shorinryukarate.club). He also serves on the Board of Advisers for Shorin Ryu Karate Do International (srkdi.com).

Printed in Great Britain
by Amazon